Understanding The Bible

Understanding The Bible

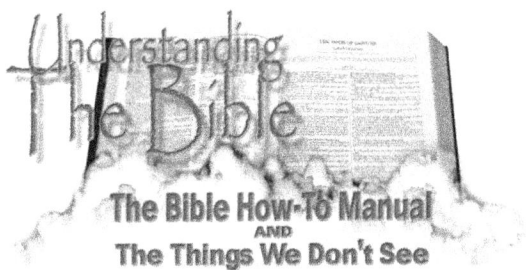

Understanding The Bible

The Bible How-To Manual
AND
The Things We Don't See

R Lindemann

Aleph Publications
Wisconsin, USA

Aleph Publications
Manitowoc WI

Paperback Edition
ISBN13: 978-1-956814-34-7

33 32 31 30 29 28 27 26 25 24   2 3 4 5 6

Disclaimer

All information, views, thoughts, and opinions expressed herein are those of the author(s) and are being presented only for your consideration and should not be interpreted as advice to take any action. Any action you take with regard to implementing or not implementing the information, views, thoughts, and opinions contained within this published work is your own responsibility. Under no circumstances are distributor(s) and/or publisher(s) and/or author(s) of this work liable for any of your actions.

Anyone, especially those who have been victim of misdirected explanation and understanding, may be best served seeking wise counsel before deciding to implement any information, views, thoughts, opinions, or anything else that is offered for your consideration in this work. All information, views, thoughts, and opinions in this work are not advice, directive, recommendation, counsel, or any other indication for anyone to take any action. All information, views, thoughts, and opinions offered herein are offered only as suggestions for your personal consideration, which is done of your own free will. Your life is your own responsibility; use it wisely.

Any use of trade names or mention of commercial sources is for informational purposes only and does not imply endorsement or affiliation.

Please note that most of the items in quotes in this book are from various versions of the Bible and have been paraphrased.

Dedication

To all who thirst for Truth and understanding, this book is dedicated to you. Your quest to know Truth is your greatest asset!

Contents

Acknowledgements

To all of you who have put your thoughts out publicly in honest books and documentaries from ages past and from present, thank you for your efforts and your thoughts. Without the thoughts of those who came before us, much of what we understand today would not be known.

Introduction

There are a few different levels of Understanding the Bible depending upon what it is you are trying to get out of Bible. This book helps to clear the fog that blocks us from understanding what is said in the many books that comprise the Bible.

Some readers of the Bible will pick it up and read the first chapter of Genesis and then never read another word from the Bible. Some of this has to do with our busy day-to-day schedules, but all too often it has more to do with the words we read and how we understood those words.

The Bible is perhaps the most intriguing book that any person can read due to its many levels of study. We can study the spiritual side, we can study the science side, we can study the historical side, we can study the meta-physical side, and we can study the theological side. With all of the targeted areas of study, perhaps the most important to most people is that of the basic overall message of Salvation—or the Spiritual.

Most readers of the Bible don't really care to *study* the Bible, but rather, simply want to read it to get the general overall message. But if you lack certain information, then your basic interpretation will be off due the misinformation that you have already heard from other sources before you read the Bible. When we combine the messages about the Bible that we are told by the secular world, together with our own reading of the Bible, it often leads our thinking down a path of interpretation errors from which it is difficult for us to recover. You have likely witnessed this with college students who grew up with a Christian background, but when in class, they were challenged on their beliefs by their professors and were unable to properly defend their position, causing them to subsequently abandon their faith due to the humiliation they faced at the hand of their professor. It is truly a sad situation when this occurs because there is no reason that any student should lack a sound Biblical base when they have been raised in a Christian environment. But due to their lack of understanding, sadly, there are very few Christians who can stand against secular scrutiny when challenged.

Our inability to properly support the Bible is mostly due to the fact that many of us do not properly grasp the Bible's history and translation nuances seen from translation to translation. There are clear answers that solve most of the issues we encounter when questioning Biblical topics, but all too often those answers are obscured by bad information, or, as is more common, a lack of information.

Getting a grasp on the basic history of the Bible's assembly and its translation trails is really quite easy. If you are doing any studying of the Bible, then it is critically important for you to first understand the major points set forth in this book.

When embarking on a quest to learn about the Bible and whether it is real, or if it is just a bunch of made up stories, you could potentially arrive at an inaccurate conclusion depending upon which Bible version you choose to read. So, in this book you will be guided through the basic history of the assembly of the Bible and offered hints on some things to be kept in mind while reading various Bible versions.

The Bible has been studied for thousands of years and its books have been debated for thousands of years, and yet, we still cannot seem to agree on some of its meaning. That means that each person is responsible, to themselves and for themselves, to undertake understanding the Bible on their own. If you choose to depend upon some preacher or a Bible group, then expect to find flaws in your rationale for why you believe what you believe.

This does not make those who you hear to be incorrect, but if you only repeat their words without properly understanding those words, then you are certain to suffer the perils of the Christian college students spoken of earlier.

It is up to each one of us to properly understand the Bible. It is indifferent regarding this book as to whether or not you choose to believe what you read in the Bible, because that is a choice only you can make and has no bearing on the actual accuracy of the text of the Bible. But I can assure you that the way you interpret the Bible will have an enormous impact on whether or not you will believe it to be accurate and true, or altogether doubt it.

It doesn't matter what you or I think, the Bible text is either true or it is not. And, as we make our decisions regarding our beliefs about the Bible's accuracy, if our decision is based upon faulty information as we begin our quest, then we are certain to end that quest with faulty conclusions.

It can take decades to discover some of the points in the Bible that you will read here in this book *Understanding The Bible*. In Our quest to discover some of these things, we learn a great deal, but often by the time we learn what you are about to read in this book, we have already hardened our beliefs to a point that even though the Truth stands before our very own eyes, we refuse to acknowledge it.

This book will not tell you what to believe, but it will set you on a path of Biblical understanding that is difficult to accomplish without coming to realize the basic information within that has been gleaned from the Bible and a few other sources.

It is my hope that in reading this book you will have a much clearer view of the Bible's text as you begin your quest to understand it. This book is not here to tell you what to believe, it is here to shed some light on aspects of Biblical research that few people know, aspects that can send you on an unforgettable journey of knowledge and understanding.

The Bible's text has been scrutinized for over two-thousand years and still has not been proven to be false. There are some minor discrepancies, but they are few in number and not particularly important. This is quite impressive since in science we frequently prove something to be false in only a matter of a couple of years, causing it to eventually fade away because the science "discovery" is no longer found to be credible.

Never go into a research project with your mind made up. Be prepared to open your mind, for if you do not, then there is little point in reading the Bible at all.

Chapter 1

The Bible - Basic Concepts

The Bible–What is it? Is it true? Is it just a bunch of fairytales? Can we trust it? Should we trust it? Who wrote the Bible? And, what does "BIBLE" mean anyway?

If someone says "Bible", you instantly know exactly what they are referring to. Many people have great reverence for the Bible. In fact, many people have great reverence for the term "bible", but they generally don't really understand what that term actually means or from where it comes. Additionally, many of us have an underlying belief that the Bible is a single written work, even though we readily acknowledge that there are many "books" within it. So, what is so special about this particular stack of paper that often stirs up such controversy and contention between those who discuss it? And, just what does the word "Bible" mean?

Before we dive into details about the Bible, we all have to come to each our own understanding about the things that we each choose to read and follow, and therefore believe. Any information that you read becomes information that will be stored in your mind, and that stored information will affect what you choose to believe about any future information that you receive. But what you choose to believe about that information has no relevance as to whether or not the information is actually correct. Being correct or *accurate* is really what we should each be concerned about. Any information, views, thoughts, and opinions you read here are not advice, directive, recommendation, counsel, or any other indication for you to take any action. For instance, the views, thoughts, and opinions offered here are offered only as suggestions for you to consider. *You* then have to think about these things and decide for yourself if they are valid and worthy of your consideration. Any Bible scholar that tries to *demand* that you believe what *they* say is true, is not a particularly credible person. If you have doubts about certain information, then it is up to you to study each side of the discussion and decide for yourself what is likely true and what is likely false. But again, the fact that we made a conclusion does not make that conclusion correct if that conclusion is actually wrong.

Concept of the Name "Bible"

The term "Bible" is derived from the Greek term "Byblos", which is typically translated as our modern term "Book". This makes sense, but it still lacks a deeper or maybe simpler understanding. What we really want to know is what the root term "Byblos" actually means.

Byblos is the name of an ancient city on the coast along the Mediterranean Sea. The meanings of ancient city names can be difficult to determine because ancient cities were often named after a person whose group or family settled in that particular spot. The meaning of those names is a topic in itself, and in our case in this book *Understanding The Bible*, knowing that won't be of much assistance in understand the origins of the name "Bible". Knowing that the term "Bible" comes from the term

"Byblos" is an important start in understanding what word "Bible" really means to us.

Why would someone name this "Bible" book after an obscure city called "Byblos"? The reason that we call it a *Bible* or *Byblos* is because the main export from the Mediterranean coastal city *Byblos* was *Papyrus*. But what has the export of *papyrus* to do with the *Bibles* we read today?

The association of *papyrus* and the *Bible* becomes clear when you find out that *papyrus* is where our modern term "paper" is derived from. In days long past, long papyrus fiber strands were stripped off of the papyrus plants and those fibrous strands were then laid down parallel and overlapping. Then an additional layer was laid down perpendicular or crossways on top of the first layer in the same parallel overlapping manner. This sticky fibrous material was wetted and pressed and then left to dry, making a flexible sheet that could be used to write on.

The first papyrus is believed to have been used in ancient Egypt roughly two- to three-thousand years before the birth of Jesus The Christ (2000-3000 BC). Because the assembled *papyrus* sheets came from the city *Byblos*, any collection of text written on such sheets would likely have been referred to as *Byblos*, like saying *book*. This term has likely been used long before the "Bible" as we know it today was collectively assembled using important ancient writings—roughly seventeen hundred years ago.

Paper, in our modern, era is extremely inexpensive relative to the labor that was needed thousands of years ago to hand-lay papyrus into sheet form to be used for writing. This hand-laid method made papyrus sheet very costly and would have only been seen as affordable by those who had sufficient purpose to record information on it. This would have mostly limited papyrus-sheet use to administrative duties of government, business, and religious entities where the recording of information is important to the infrastructure of the particular entity.

If we were to be naming the "Bible" in the same manner today, we would likely be naming it something to the order of "Appleton" or "Wisconsin" because that city and state are top producers and shippers of paper in our modern times.

Paper or *papyrus* is what the Bible is written on, and *Bible* or *Byblos* is the city from which the paper is exported. The reason that the term *Byblos* or *Bible* has endured, is because The Holy Bible is the one single set of documents that has been carried through thousands of years on this *papyrus* or *paper* form of material that we still read today. The earliest assembly of the Bible was likely referred to as "Byblos" or "Vyvlos", or something that sounded very close to that, for well over two-thousand years. There are two important aspects of a Bible: The first is that the Bible is *not* a stack of blank paper, rather it is a thick stack of *printed* or *inscribed* paper. And the second and more important aspect is what that inscription or printing actually says.

Grasping the Magnitude

You can walk into any library and see tens of thousands of books on the shelves, books that no one really cares much about or pays any attention to. And many of those books had only a single print-run of a few thousand books. The Bible, on the other hand, has been translated into nearly every language on Earth and has been printed and reprinted in print-runs of millions over and over and over again.

It is estimated that there are over 100 million Bibles printed worldwide *every year*. To get a grasp on this quantity, you must realize that the average weight of a Bible is roughly two and a half pounds when averaging both the smaller and larger Bibles. A typical semi-trailer can carry only about 16,000 Bibles per load. At over 100 million Bibles per year, that is over 5900 semi-trailers filled with brand new Bibles *every year* that are being distributed, and that is not considering online Bibles.

Grasp the Assembly

Now that we understand why the "Bible" is named as it is and the magnitude of its distribution, we need to get a grasp on how it came about. When we consider how the Bible got its name, we have to realize that any other book could have been named similarly, which would be confusing to us, yet this is not the case.

The "Bible" is unique in that it is the only book that is specifically called by that name. In some languages the "b" and "v" sounds are interchanged. In Greek, "Bible" or "Byblios", is pronounced "veevleeos", and "Book" is pronounced "veevleeo". In other words, "The Bible" is *the paper stack* or "The Book".

Many of us have the erred belief that the Bible was written all at one time by some group of priests long ago, or maybe that the Bible is some sort of document that God personally handed to Moses along with the Ten Commandments on Mount Sinai. But the Bible is actually a set of historical books that were assembled over a long period of thousands of years.

There is a lot of speculation of who wrote what, and when they did it regarding the Bible. If you dive into the realm of Bible scholars, you will find that much of their so-called "*knowledge*" on the subject is actually their *opinion* on the writers and the estimated dates of writings found in the Bible. And amongst those scholars there are many opinions that are often in conflict with the opinions of their peers regarding the books in the Bible. The general rule of thumb here is that there are as many opinions as there are scholars. If a "Bible Scholar" says that the Bible is divinely inspired, then you can be sure that there is another scholar who insists that it is not.

When trying to grasp the assembly of the Bible, we are often forced to disregard the scholarly opinions and set out on our own quest of discovery. But let us not disregard some of what they have discovered. If a Bible scholar can offer you source material with which you can arrive at your own opinion, then that source material may actually have value to you.

Bible scholars study the writing of the Bible and the basis of the text, but they generally don't touch on the scientific aspects, and often don't even do much regarding the historical aspects of *the contents of the text*, though some do.

It is the historical aspects that are perhaps the most important to understand when trying to wrap our minds around the Bible and its composition. The Bible is a history of a very specific group of people who recorded their political and personal triumphs and follies. They recorded this information as it occurred, or shortly thereafter, and then added to it when additional noteworthy events occurred.

Some of the books may have been written at a later date as an effort to be recompiled in a more succinct format for brevity and clarity. Yet, most books in the Bible appear to have been written just after the fact, and some even as an instruction at the time of the stated visitation, such as the text of some of the prophets' books. This assembly of documentation continued until the epistles in the New Testament, at which point writings were no longer added to the Bible as we know it today. As writings were penned they were dutifully carried along for centuries by these people. Some of the books in the Bible may have been additions to a stack of previously written books comprising parts of the current Bible as those additional books were collected from different groups within the people of which the Bible is a record of.

There is no *definitive* answer as to exactly when and by whom the writings were done, and there likely never will be. But regardless of our inability to determine the actual authors and dates that each text was penned, it is not really as important as is the question of whether or not the text is *accurate* and *true*.

The book we call "The Bible" has been highly favored by many people for over two-thousand years, and parts of the Old Testament for about three-thousand years. For many people, the Bible is not just any book, rather it is *The* Book. It is now, and always has been a book with special meaning to many people, especially Jews and Christians. The Bible, or Scriptures as it is often referred to, also have special meaning to many Muslims who take the time to actually read it and their Quran together.

Chapter 2

What Evidence Exists

What is so special about the Bible? And does evidence exist that can answer the question: "Is the Bible true?" To answer the questions, we must first place our focus on a couple of other questions which are: What is *Truth*? And what exactly do we mean by "Is the Bible true?"

Pontius Pilot asked Christ "What is Truth?"

Apparently, this question of "What is Truth?" has been asked for a very long time. According to the Bible, Jesus The Christ said "Everyone that is of the truth hears my voice." To which Pontius Pilot responded "What is Truth?" When you understand Truth, then the question "What is Truth?" sounds like a silly question. Yet there are many of us who simply do not grasp, or maybe admit to, the basic concept of Truth. Some people even go as far as to claim that "truth" is to each of us whatever we choose to believe.

We often confuse the question "What is Truth?" with the question "What is true?", and there is a very big difference between these two questions. If you have not understood that this difference exists, then you *will* struggle in any research you do on any topic. You truly cannot ever know what is true if you fail to understand what *Truth* is. This is perhaps the most prominent reason that the Bible invokes so much debate on both sides regarding the "Is the Bible true?" question.

We inherently all know what Truth is, but we choose to ignore that understanding in order to continue in either what we have been taught to believe, or in what we choose to believe. Make a distinction in your mind *before* you study the Bible as to which is which. Doing so will allow you to more readily see what is true and what is not true.

When you confuse these two questions, what is *truth* versus what is *true*, it is quite common to wind up following foolish theology theories that are inconsistent with the actual thoughts and sentiment that are intended to be conveyed in the Bible's text. It's easy to be led astray by false preachers when you are unaware of the distinction between *what Truth is* versus *what is true*. You might think by saying "false preachers" that I am referring to those who preach the Bible inaccurately but yet are still preaching of God, and I am. But in the saying "false preachers", I am also including those who espouse views that defy the Bible on any basis that can be thought up, but which are in fact *not* correct views.

Anyone who is promoting anything that is not of truth is a "false preacher" of that which they are promoting. False preachers are abundant in religious and in secular circles. What we need to decide for ourselves is, will we believe those false preachers without verification? Or will we check their claims to see if those claims are consistent with general and Biblical history, with true science, and with basic logic?

What is True?

The question "What is true?" differs from "What is Truth?" in that it is asking about a specific subject and if that event actually occurred. Where asking "What is Truth?", on the other hand, is specifically pondering what the concept of "Truth" is. When we discuss the Bible, we are typically asking "What is true?" So if we ask "Is the Bible true?", then what we are seeking to know is, what **Is**. In other words, we wonder: Did the events as described in the Bible actually occur as stated?

So then, how do we determine if the events in the Bible are true? You could ask many Christians, and typically they will say "Yes, the events in the Bible are true", and when you further question them they convey a sentiment such as, "The Bible said it, so it has to be true." While there is some merit to this, it is really a dangerous way to understand the Bible. With such rationale, someone could invent any theory and then say that the theory itself proves the theory to be true. This is similar to big bang theology, where the theory of big bang is the evidence that the big bang is real. That debate is discussed in the *The Science of God* Series and in *Bending The Ruler*.

Interestingly, there are many ex-Christians who now espouse the same the-Bible-told-me-so rationale in their newly adopted big bang theologies, but this methodology is not of Truth. To drill down to Truth, we must dispose of our own predispositions that force us to stay on our comfortable paths of error. We must live in the text to better understand it.

Living In the Text

"Living in the text" is not you becoming like the text, or believing the text, or anything more than investigating the text as if it is possibly true. If you have decided that the text is "just a bunch of stories", then you cannot "live in the text" because you have already decided that the text is not true and therefore it is almost certain that you will not pursue any evidence proving it to be true. It might not be that you are specifically ignoring the evidence, but rather that you will not recognize it because you have basically discounted it. This is like the-red-car-effect that I speak of in several of my books. In the-red-car-effect you typically won't notice red cars until you buy a red car, and once you own a red car you then suddenly notice them everywhere you look. The cars have always been there, but you now notice them because *you* are conditioned to recognize them.

A similar but opposite effect occurs when you have religious perspectives that are biased where you will read the text the way you have been *taught* to read and understand the text. When we live *outside* of the text in these ways, we suffer from red-car-blindness. So, while the red-car-effect can help us to recognize red cars, it also can negatively affect our view of other non-red cars, thus causing them to be outside of our focus and field of view.

Red cars are somewhat unique since most cars are blend-in blues, blacks, and grays. If you have a blend-in-sort-of-car-color you will sometimes notice cars that are identical to yours, but generally they drive right past you without any notice from you. The text of the Bible works much this way, where if you have a mundane Christian understanding of the text, then all cars look the same as your common colored car because they blend in. So, to you, all Bible text looks like your mundane Christian perspective of the text.

If you happen to be a believer of certain specific teachings about the Bible, then those red-car teachings, being unique in nature, will stand out to you when you come across them as you read the text. Yet, if you have decided in your mind that your special red-car text *is the only way*, then you will also tend to overlook the mundane text as you enthusiastically examine your unique red-car type text. Your mission is to remove these blindnesses. This includes both the mundane blindness and the narrow red-car view. Become aware of the red-car text, but don't develop too focused of a view on it or you won't be able to see the Biblical forest through the Biblical trees. Back up from your perspective and try to see the *overall* view of the Bible and its text, because it is very different than most people think or want to believe.

Chapter 3

Here's Some Good News

To get a grasp on the Bible, we first have to understand a few things about it. Unless you can grasp some of what you will read here, you are likely to blur many critical aspects of the Bible, making it almost impossible for you to properly understand much of it.

But even if you do not understand the things that are discussed in this book, *Understanding The Bible*, you should still be able to easily extract the most critical aspect of the Bible, which is the message of "Salvation" that we often hear people speak about. In fact, to understand Salvation, you generally only need to read the Gospels. However, reading only the Gospels will not enable you to engage in intelligible discussion with others on most Biblical topics, which is one of Christianity's most prominent problems.

The term "Gospel" is *God* or *Good* plus the word *Spell*, or to write out or tell. "Gospel" basically means *God-* or *Good-Tell*, and when we *tell* someone something, we often first say "Did you hear the good news?", and then we proceed to share the story.

Thus, the Gospels are the "Good News". But this book, *Understanding The Bible*, is not about Salvation, so you won't find preaching about being saved here, though it is explained when needed for informational purposes. Instead, you are going to read information that is typically *not* heard or *understood* by most people. And it is this lack of understanding that causes us to struggle with many topics surrounding the Bible.

When it comes to any details that challenge our faith, most of us are at a complete loss to refute those challenges. Some of the challenges are good and true, meaning that we must change our own erred views. Yet often, while our views are correct, we still lack an ability to adequately defend those views but we force our challengers to rethink *their* own perspective. When Christian's are publicly challenged, it is typically a humiliating experience for them. Most Christians hold tightly to their blind faith, never able to adequately defend the text of the Bible upon which they base that blind faith. Thus, if anyone can undermine the Bible in your mind, then that upon which you base your blind-faith will be discredited in your own mind as we often see happen with college students when they abandon their religion.

Whenever a person enters a journey to learn anything, their perception of the evidence that they find will be affected by the information they have previously heard and believed *before* embarking on that journey. Understanding this about yourself can help you to clear your view *before* you begin reading or studying the Bible.

If you enter into any level of Bible reading or Bible study with *any* agenda whatsoever, then that agenda *will* be fulfilled for you. Clearing our view of agenda can open many doors of learning for us. The Bible is a book that is overflowing with information, and some of that information is good, and some of it harsh, but much of the information is confusing to most of us. It all depends upon what we go into it with. The only agenda that we should ever have is to always seek Truth and find out what is true. This is true of anything we study, whether Biblical or non-Biblical.

Many Christians read the Bible through their rose-colored glasses, where many scientists and atheists, on the other hand, read the Bible though their godless opaque-black glasses. But seldom do we see people read the Bible through the crystal-clear lenses of Truth–if they read the Bible at all.

You will see the term "godless" in this book, but it is not intended as a dig or insult in any way. Rather, it indicates that there is a distinct difference between a godless-perspective and a God-perspective when reading the Bible. "Godless" simply means that someone's perspective is void of a god-influenced mentality and viewpoint. A *Christian* approach and a *godless* approach will certainly arrive at different conclusions after having read the Bible.

Opaque Black Glasses

When we read books by atheists or scientists, or hear them speak, it is typically very apparent that if they read the Bible at all, they only read it through opaque-black glasses. Yet, when pressed on their interpretation, they generally claim to have done so objectively. Far too often we hear this opaque-black-glasses group railing against the Bible, stating that "The Bible is just a bunch of made up stories." Or "The Bible is all myth."

Is it true? Is the Bible just a bunch of made up stories? And exactly where did those opaque-black glasses come from? The atheist approach is often shared by those in the various science fields. You will see this most prominently in the areas of astrophysics and biological-evolution. Most of those who share the godless view have been raised in godless families, or are from Christian families that failed to properly fill their children in on the adult details of the Bible.

Many Christian families will read a Children's Bible to their children when the children are young, but then fail to continue teaching their children as the children become adults. With the Bible being a very long book, it is typically not particularly appealing to young adults, and thus their Biblical learning never really advances beyond a Children's Bible perspective.

It is Christian children who had not been given proper details of the Bible as they age who tend to abandon the Bible when they are challenged in college. The humiliation that many Christian students experience when they get beat down in debate causes them to close their eyes to the Bible. And it is they who then also adopt a godless view of the Bible as they enter the various scientific fields as they are fitted for their new godless opaque-black glasses. Some of these godless scientists and atheists are well-read scholars and have, as adults, studied the Bible. But many, if not most, have not studied the Bible as older adults. This means that the Biblical education that many people have is only on the Children's Bible level, which is a rose-colored rendition of the Bible.

Rose Colored Glasses

If you are a rose-colored glasses Christian, then buckle up because the Bible is *not* what you might like to think it is. It's common for Christians to view the Bible through their rose-colored glasses, in fact, not only is it common, it is almost certain that this is the case for *most* Christians. But while the Bible speaks much of love and Salvation, especially in the New Testament, the Bible is *not* all rainbows and lollipops!

There are many stories in the Bible that have become endearing tales that we love to share with our children. But when you read through those same accounts from an adult's version of the Bible and you do so with a young child on your lap, you won't get very far before realizing that you might need to filter some of the information *before* you speak it out loud to those unprepared little ears.

Sure, the Bible is full of love and Joy, but it is also full of murder and adultery and deceit and, and, and…, but do not let this detour you from researching it. While the Bible is full of deceit it is not the text that is deceitful, rather the text is telling about people's lies and deceit and murders and adultery etc, as well as their triumphs. This is why we have "Children's Bibles". Children are not prepared to hear of the atrocities that we foolish adults commit against one another, so we have tamped them down to be a bit more child-friendly than they actually are.

This is both a good and a bad thing. It's good because it teaches the children some of the better points in history and of perseverance and heroes etc., yet it can be bad. Why bad? It is bad because we, as parents, fail to continue to teach our children about the larger lessons in the Bible. We might read our children the Bible stories while they're young, but then as they age, we fail to fill them in on the, let's call them, "adult details" of the Bible. This Children's Bible situation then leaves them with a rose-colored-glasses view of the Bible, thinking that is it all about rainbows and animals and love etc. This rose-colored view is then enhanced by many preachers that they encounter and by Christian schools they might attend, but this rose-colored view is very difficult to defend when you do not properly understand the other parts of the Bible. This rose-colored view is also further supported by those who claim that the Bible is nothing more than mere fables.

But Christians are not the only ones who need to have their Biblical vision checked. Many people of science and also atheists are no better. Our rose-colored lenses can quickly turn to black when we are challenged but lack the details offered by the crystal-clear lenses of Truth.

Crystal Clear Glasses of Truth

Why is it so difficult for us to find our crystal-clear glasses of Truth? Sadly, it's because those who teach us tend to wear either the opaque-black glasses of "science", or they wear the rose-colored glasses of religion. They are therefore incapable of teaching us to wear only the crystal-clear glasses of Truth in *any* area of study. You have to be deliberately ignorant to not look around and see these extreme biases on both sides of the Bible feuds.

Is the Bible a rose-colored book or maybe book of solid-black, and our glasses are perfectly clear? Or have we chosen our favorite colored glasses to suit our own desires and understanding of the Bible?

The Bible, while perhaps the most informative and honest account of humanity, is anything but a rose-colored book. And it is filled with scientific information that cannot be seen when wearing the opaque-black glasses of science *or* the rose-colored glasses of religion.

People often lose their rose-colored glasses when they are struggling in life while seeking answers as certain things are pointed out to them, such as the fact that the Bible is full of murder and adultery and deception. If you have not come to understand the Bible, this is typically a point were turning away from the Bible feels more comfortable, because we then don't have to face our own fault in our own troubles.

Getting a good grasp on the truth about the Bible and its accuracy, or inaccuracy, demands that we cast away our old colored glasses that have tainted our view for so long, and then replace them with the crystal-clear glasses of Truth. And *that* is your quest: To study, or even just read the text of the Bible through the crystal-clear lenses of Truth.

Chapter 4

Finding Your Way Through The Bible

Once we have removed the blinders of our preferred rose or black color glasses, we can then begin an objective journey to see if the Bible is worthy of our time. Why do we even bother with this contentious book? While we might not realize it, the Bible and its contents are deeply interwoven in nearly every part of western culture. There is probably no one over the age of ten who has been raised in western culture that has not at least heard of the Bible at some point. And there is certainly not a single person who has not been affected by it in western culture. In fact, the majority of people on the entire globe who are over the age of ten generally have had at least a minute level of introduction to the Bible, even if only in its name. It is estimated that there have been enough Bibles printed for every adult on Earth to each have one.

The reason we bother with the Bible is because there are those who say that it is all fables, yet here we are in our western culture influenced by this book of supposed "fables" or "myths" in nearly every facet of our lives. We also have countless instances of people who were struggling with tough life-circumstances and feeling lost who happened to stumble upon some preacher yacking about God and the Bible blah blah blah... when suddenly something that the preacher says hits home and piques their curiosity. It is these things that make us stop and ask if maybe it is all real and true—and thus our quest begins!

But, once you begin to dive in to trying to understand what the Bible is all about, you will soon run into two basic views. The first is the rose-colored view that the Bible is the "inerrant inspired word of God". And the second is the opaque-black view that "the Bible is a bunch of fables that were made up by religious leaders to frighten people so that they could control them." *Your* quest is to decide which if either of these two views is correct—or is there maybe another choice? We'll get into all of this later, but first let's examine if the Bible is a book of mere "fables".

Biblical Fables

If you read or watch enough material that comes out of the worlds of atheism and "science", you are certain to hear statements such as, "The Bible is just a bunch of stories someone created to scare people." But let us examine just who it is that is creating stories. Is it the writers of the Bible? Or is it those who refute the Bible? Or who?

The Bible is a very diverse book regardless of whether or not it's all true. In considering if it is true, there are levels of content or truth to be considered. One level is, did the events occur as described? And another level is, are the sentiments or lessons true or good?

The books of the Bible are all written as if the events in them actually occurred, but within some of those written accounts there are stories being told which are not true in that they did not actually occur, and when they are told, it is typically obvious that these are fables being used as examples. Such stories are referred to as "parables". Parables were used by Jesus when he was talking to people. The parables were lessons The Christ was conveying to the people. The parables he offered were a sort of analogy of their circumstances relative to God for them to achieve Salvation. But this cloaked the information for the blind listener, unless they were able to grasp the simplicity of the parables.

Then there are books such as "Proverbs" that are one-liner-type statements that can be readily applied to the lives of most people to enhance their lives. These brief statements are thought of as true points about life, yet they are *not* said to specifically have occurred as historical events in themselves. But historically, they were written by prominent persons who are included in the histories listed in some of the other books in the Bible.

One of the points to be made about the Bible is that, more than anything else, it is a book of the *history* of a line of people who carried forward the books contained within the Bible through the years up until the point where the Biblical accounts end. You might disagree with the nature of what they did and their morality, and you might disagree with the lessons contained in the parables and the Proverbs, but the history of much of the Bible cannot be denied by you if you care to be considered a credible person.

The following is an incredibly important point for you to understand regarding the Bible. The documentation from various cultures throughout the world recognize the people of the Bible to have existed in some of their own historical documentation from their respective regions. Even the Quran of the Muslims speaks of the scriptures and of the people to whom those scriptures were entrusted, namely the Jews and the Christians. To deny this information shows a great deal of ignorance. But while this history does acknowledge the people of the Bible to have undeniably existed, it does not address whether or not the specific *events* described in the Bible actually occurred.

Understanding that the Bible has historical accounts where fables or parables and proverbs were also written, can help in spotting those aspects when you come upon them in the Bible, thus allowing *you* to separate the *facts* of the Bible from the *parables* of the Bible. This works like the red-car-effect mentioned in a previous chapter. When you are *aware* of something then it becomes much easier to spot when you come across it. The New Testament tells of many times where "parables" where used, where the Old Testament has some Proverbs and other such writings.

Now that we understand that the Bible does in fact tell some stories that have been invented for the specific purpose of teaching lessons by those who are spoken of in the Bible, we can more easily recognize the parts that are speaking of actual events.

The New and The Old

Now that we know a little bit about parables and proverbs, we can look into what the deal is with these things called "Testaments", as in the *New Testament* and the *Old Testament*. What's the difference between them and what does "Testament" mean to begin with?

A "Testament" is an account given by an eye witness. The term "Old" has the obvious meaning of *aged*. And "New" means *recent*. Both of these are relative terms. Something newer than an *already new* thing makes the *already new* thing be comparatively older. Pretty simple!

"Old Testament" simply means that it was an earlier collection of books *testifying* to events that occurred. And "New Testament" is indicating that it is an addendum to the older collection of writings, with the newer having eye witness testimony to events that are more recent than the older already existing testimony. But what is it that makes the New Testament distinctly different?

The term "Bible" that we spoke of in an earlier chapter when discussing the word's origins, is often used as a general descriptive term to convey holy books from other cultures. For instance, it is fairly common to hear the Quran referred to as "the Muslims' Bible" thus conveying that the Quran is their holy book. Similarly, the same is true of the holy book of the Jews, which is often referred to as the "Jewish Bible". The "Jewish Bible" is typically referred to as the "Tanakh". The name "Tanakh" is derived from the names of the three sections of the Hebrew Bible, which are the *Torah* (the first five books), the *Nevi'im* (or prophets), and the *Ketuvim* (the writings). The peculiar spelling that we see in *Tanakh* is derived as a phonetic translation of the pronunciation of the acronym *TNK* or *T̲orah*, *N̲evi'im*, and *K̲etuvim*. It's a little bit more nuanced than that, but for our purposes here that's more than enough explanation.

What you might not have caught in the previous paragraph is the use of the term the "Hebrew Bible". This is a very important term for you to remember. The "Hebrew Bible" *is* the "Old Testament" part in the book that we typically call "The Bible". But since the *Jewish Bible*, or *Tanakh*, doesn't include the New Testament, you will generally not see the term "Old Testament" used in reference to the Jewish Bible because there is no point, because the Jews only have *one* testament.

The *New Testament* is an addition to the *Jewish* or *Hebrew Bible*, and that *New Testament* is the documentation of the awaited Savior who many believe is the Chosen Messiah–Jesus The Christ. Since the majority of Jews do not accept the man who we refer to as "Jesus" as the promised Savior, it nullifies the entire New Testament in their view, and thus they saw no logical reason to add it to the existing *Hebrew Bible*.

The distinction that you can derive from this is that the Hebrew Bible is a historical document of the Hebrew people which the Jews are a part of. The New Testament is the account of the *Birth, Life, Death, Resurrection,* and *Ascension* of the long-awaited Messiah as told in the four "Gospels", which, as you should recall, is the "Good News". The remainder of the New Testament is largely composed of letters written by Apostles or followers of the Christ. These Apostles and followers sent those letters abroad in effort to share the "Good News" as told in the Gospels. These letters are referred to as the "Epistles", which means *To Send*.

These letters or *"Epistles"* are only a part of the documentation still in existence regarding the rapid proliferation of Christianity. If you have not already noticed, take note that the word "Christ" is the prominent part of the words **Christ**ianity and **Christ**mas. The Epistles are documentation of work that was done in effort to share the "Good News", that is to say the "Gospel", with the world regarding the arrival of This Savior Christ person who was foretold in the Old Testament. And the Epistles tell of the perils and of the triumphs of that mission. Some of the Epistles were written and intended to be corrections to inaccurate doctrine that many people had heard in general conversation and teaching, or misinterpreted from a previous epistle/letter.

Chapter 5

The Inspired Word of God

A phrase that we frequently hear used by preachers is "Inspired Word Of God". But what does the "Inspired Word Of God" mean? Generally, it means that the people who wrote the words written in the various books of the Bible were inspired by God as those words were written. "Inspired" could be thought of as in**spirit**ed because the word *spirit* is where the word inspired is derived from. It basically means that the spirit is in you, or more concisely, the Spirit Of **God** is in you.

Some of the people who wrote some the books who are detailed in Bible are said to have been visited by angels or were taken away and were shown various things in visions. If we are to believe these accounts to be true, then it is easy to see how we would assume that they would have been *inspired* or *inspirited* by God, and thus that which was recorded by them is considered "inspired". But is **all** of the Bible inspired in this same way? Yes and no.

Not all of the books in the Bible are accounts of visitations by angles or visions that we would consider to have been inspired. But the people who wrote the text, or had someone write it for them, generally did at some point have some sort of visitation or vision, thus the claim can be made that those writings are indeed "inspired". There are varying views regarding the quantity of "inspired" books to be found in the Bible, ranging from the atheist's *zero books* to the blind-faithed Christian's *all books* being inspired. If these Biblical books are potentially inspired, then can they also be considered *inerrant?*

The Inerrant Word Of God

"Inerrant" is a very strong term to be used in conjunction with any account of history, and it is also a term that we commonly hear when preachers talk about the Bible. Claiming "inerrancy" is risky when considering any historical accounts, especially those that are from ancient times. Ancient written accounts typically have to be translated at some point in time in order for those of us who are alive at this moment to be able to read them. The people translating can compromise the claimed *inerrancy* of the Bible if not done with a great deal of care. Later we will be discussing a bit about the various translations and their accuracy or inerrancy.

If we are to believe that the books in the Bible are inspired, then it's easy to accept that they are also "inerrant", and of course this belief is held by those who have chosen to believe that *all* books and all parts of them in the Bible are inspired.

The inerrancy of our modern Bibles quickly comes to question when we begin to learn some history of the Bible. For instance, which specific Bible versions are inerrant? We like to put our beliefs in little pretty *mental* boxes that we carry our Bibles around in. However, when we realize that not all Bibles are created equal, we must then examine why this is so. If Bibles are perfectly "inerrant", then there should be no difference between any of them. Yet, most people who are reasonably familiar with the Bible will say that the Bible has sixty-six books. There's even a song about the Bible having sixty-six books. Even many Catholics think sixty-six books is the actual count. However, many Bibles, *especially* those used by Catholics, contain seventy-three books. Why such a discrepancy over a book that is claimed to be "inerrant"? Some of the books included in many Bibles are considered to be less authoritative, and generally it is those books that account for the difference in book quantities between the various Bibles. These books are referred to as "Biblical Apocrypha" meaning that the author and origin of the books are in question. Does this make them wrong or filled with error? No, inerrancy is different than what many people take it as.

Inerrancy

"Inerrant" has the obvious meaning of being without error. Yet in this we do have translation errors and discrepancies regarding book quantities between Bible versions. In fact, some books in the Bible contain a few extra verses or an extra chapter or two. So how then can we make the claim that the Bible is "inerrant" when they don't all match?

The Bible can be claimed to be inerrant because the original writings that are claimed to have been inspired would have by default been inerrant and thus we can say that the *original* is inerrant. And since our Bibles today are derived from those inerrant originals, our modern Bibles have inherited this claimed "inerrancy".

People are all over the spectrum regarding their belief on this particular debate about the Bible's level of inerrancy. I personally have a difficult time accepting this particular version of Biblical inerrancy as you might have gathered if you had the opportunity to read any of the various volumes of the *The Science Of God* books which clearly expose the often overreaching "inerrancy" claims.

But there is another sort of inerrancy that can be attributed to the Bible, which is that the lessons to be learned from it are good and true and are thus inerrant. With this I can readily agree provided that we are speaking only of the *good* lessons and examples. Yet, even here I struggle because there is a great deal of recorded history of people behaving badly in the Bible that *no one* should follow.

The Bible is filled with much good, and many very good lessons can be learned from it, as well as from the bad behavior of people it has recorded, but attributing inerrancy to the Bible overall, with such bad behavior as is recorded in the Bible, causes many people to turn from the Bible when they read of the murders, adultery, treachery, and hate that permeates some of the accounts recorded in the Bible. When we claim Biblical inerrancy, it confuses people who finally sit down to read the Bible. Yet, if those accounts of murders, adultery, treachery, and hate are true and accurate, then that again would speak for the inerrancy of the Bible.

We each must arrive at our own assessment of the Bible's claimed inerrancy, but that assessment is largely going to be determined by which particular inerrancy rationale we chose to use. *You* will have to decide this on your own. For myself, I feel that while the Bible was likely written as documentation of events of the time and was likely accurately so done, there have since been some translations that we cannot call "inerrant" today. Yet, the lessons, when not perverted by our biases and failures to admit our own faults, are really quite accurate and therefore can be claimed as "inerrant".

So, while the Bible is largely inerrant, there are issues with that thought. You must always keep in mind that most of the potential flaws in the suggested "inerrancy" have to do with our own interpretation and translation of the text. Inerrancy has nothing to do with God. God is said to be perfect and thus inerrant. You could write you own biography to perfection, and provided that you make no errors, your book could then be considered "inerrant". Inerrant is not some magical formula that the Bible possesses, it is merely a statement of accuracy which we will be getting into when discussing a few specifics about the various versions.

Do not let this issue of inerrancy or potential faults detour you from diving into reading or studying the Bible. Just the historical value of the contents alone is without price, and is very informative and should be known by all.

In reading the *The Science of God* volumes, you will quickly see that this inerrancy issue can be a big point of contention depending upon how you understand "inerrancy", and it also depends upon which Bible versions you choose to read or use for study. Inerrant is a point of perfection that some modern Bible versions **cannot** legitimately claim. However, most versions are very accurate when allowing for some minor error. These possible errors should not turn us away from the Bible; Instead, it should make us curious as to which specific statements are not accurate and why that might be.

If we have the crystal-clear glasses of truth in hand, then we should put them on and find those potential translation errors that might exist in some Bible versions, and then look beyond them to find the truth or the accurate account of what was originally written.

Chapter 6

Combining with or Adding to The Bible

When diving into reading the Bible or studying it, you will often hear "Whoever adds to or takes away from the Bible" will suffer the plagues described in the book of Revelation, or they will have their share taken from the Tree of Life etc. But this is often misunderstood as being in reference to the Bible overall, which it is not. This is a specific reference to something said in the book of Revelation chapter twenty-two, and it pertains specifically to the book of Revelation *only*. Often, people who are from the protestant side of the Reformation divide wrongly apply this statement to the inclusion of the Biblical Apocrypha books that many Bibles, including Catholic Bibles, contain. But again, the statement "Whoever adds to or takes away from the Bible" is not a proper quote and is really from and for the book of Revelation. The Douay Rheims version Chapter 22 puts it this way: "For I testify to everyone that hears the words of the prophecy of this book: If any man shall add to these things, God shall add unto him the plagues written in this book. And if any man shall take away from the words of the book of this prophecy, God shall take away his part out of the book of life, and out of the holy city, and from these things that are written in this book."

So do not fear if you read one of the extended versions of the Bible, such as the Douay Rheims version, for you will not burst into flames or suddenly become a Catholic if you read these Biblical Apocryphal books. They contain interesting information that, if you are studying the Bible, you will eventually want to and likely need to know.

Biblical Apocrypha

What does "apocrypha" mean? Apocrypha comes from a similar sounding Greek word meaning *secret,* or *to hide,* or *hidden,* or *not known.* Referred to as the "deuterocanonical" books by the Catholic Church, the Biblical Apocryphal books are books that either could not be well documented as to their original author and authenticity, *or* they are books that have a hidden meaning—indicating that they are difficult to understand. Even in the simple word *apocrypha* there is controversy within the Biblical circles.

Some or all of the Biblical Apocrypha are included in the Septuagint, the Latin Vulgate Bible, the Douay Rheims Bible, and some others. At one time, even the Original King James Bible included the Biblical Apocrypha, but the Biblical Apocrypha is typically not found in the Hebrew Bible, that is to say the *Tanakh.* We know that the Biblical Apocrypha is verifiably old and is respected and studied by many scholars, even Jewish scholars respect it, even though those writings are not included in their Hebrew Bible canon. These apocryphal books are typically not included in most modern protestant Bibles. The Biblical Apocryphal books were a part of the King James Bible for over 270 years until they were removed in the 1880s. The names of these books are as follow:

1. 1 Esdras - Vulgate 3 Esdras
2. 2 Esdras - Vulgate 4 Esdras
3. Tobit
4. Judith

5. Esther
6. Wisdom
7. Ecclesiasticus - also known as Sirach
8. Baruch
9. Song of the Three Children - Daniel 3:24–90
10. Story of Susanna - Daniel 13
11. The Idol Bel and the Dragon - Daniel 14
12. Prayer of Manasseh - Daniel
13. 1 Maccabees
14. 2 Maccabees

The Canon

You have likely noticed the use of the words "Canon" and "deuterocanonical". What is the Biblical "Canon"? *Canon* is a *general law* or *rule* that we use to judge things by, and thus the principles found in the Bible are the "canon". *Canon* is from an identical sounding Greek word meaning to *measure*. The use of the term "Canon" is in essence saying: As a people, these are our rules that we choose to follow. "**Canon**ical" is simply an indication that it is a part of the canon. A particular Bible version that is the primary source of any one religion is the canon of that religious division. The Hebrew canon does not include the apocrypha, nor does the Protestant canon. However, the Catholic canon does.

The term "deuterocanonical" means *second canon*, Greek "deuteros" means *two* or *second*. This term is used because, while the Hebrew Bible does not include these books, the Septuagint canon that ascended from it did include those in the Old Testament time-line. There is a truly interesting stack of information about all of this, but it is not a topic for this book as it can get quite detailed. Knowing these basics will help if you get deep into the study of the Bible, and you will certainly enjoy learning about these and other ancient books or texts.

While the term *canon* can be used outside of Biblical purposes, it is in the study of the Bible where you will typically find the term used.

Pseudepigrapha

Another word you might hear when studying the Bible is "Pseudepigrapha" which means *falsely attributed to*. The intended meaning here is that it is uncertain who originally penned these works. They are generally not considered Biblical apocrypha but are read by most Bible scholars. When diving into the hair-splitting aspects of Biblical or historical books, there are several categories of authenticity that are used. These categories are grouped into the following groups: First is the Bible books that everyone agrees on which are found in **all** Bibles or "canons" of the people. The next is the list of Biblical apocryphal books or deuterocanonical books mentioned in the last section. Then there is the pseudepigrapha that have uncertain authors and are *not* included in any Bibles. Some of those books are as follows:

1. Apocalypse of Abraham
2. Books of Adam and Eve
3. Apocalypse of Adam
4. Syriac Apocalypse of Baruch
5. Biblical Antiquities
6. Book of Enoch
7. Book of the Secrets of Enoch
8. Fourth Book of Ezra (2 Esdras)
9. Books of Giants
10. Book of Jubilees
11. Lives of the Prophets
12. Fourth Book of Maccabees
13. Testament of Moses
14. Sibylline Oracles
15. Testament of Solomon
16. Testaments of the Twelve Patriarchs

As you can see, there is a bit more to it all than just picking up a Bible and reading it and then suddenly being a "Bible expert". The part of Bible study that is a true joy is when *you* can make connections that others have not realized or that they do not discuss, and/or when you have revelations of your own about something in the text that you can share with others.

The issues in this chapter have been discussed and debated for thousands of years. But while the debates are many, we all need to realize that the debate is not *if* the books being discussed in this chapter and all of the other books in the Bible have value. The debate is now, and always has been, the *level* of value that any non-canonical books have. These extra books are very interesting, to say the least. However, foolish people sometimes will take some of these extra books which might have questionable origins and then they cast away the entire Biblical Canon and build false beliefs upon the questionable books along with their own inaccurate interpretation of the those books/texts.

Some of these extra books are fragmented, so someone trying to build doctrine from them is indeed foolish. Imagine if the Constitution of The United States of America was fragmented: We produce millions of perfect **complete** copies of it every year, and yet we can't even agree on that simple, beautiful, and brief document in all of its fullness. So, it is utter fantasy for anyone to imagine that we humans would not build foolish and false doctrine upon books that are *fragmented* or are of questionable authorship and are very old.

I would rather not have had to mention this chapter about the extra books, but it is one of the first things a person often runs into when first inquiring about the Bible. Sometimes we grab a Bible that someone gave to us and begin reading it, then when we question something that we just read, we go to look it up somewhere and suddenly we are launched into the gray area of the extra books discussed in this chapter.

In initial readings and study of the Bible, it is best to not dwell on these extra books until the dust from reading the main part of the Bible has settled in your mind. After that, these books tend to have much more significance to any reader of them or of the Bible. Work to separate the topics in your mind, because if we fail to properly separate these issues, it tends to cloud the mind.

Chapter 7

Separating the Topics

What is the benefit of separating topics? When I talk about "separating topics", I'm referring to being able to create mental divisions between general points of interests. For instance, many people, if not most, connect God and religion, yet God really has nothing to do with religion at all, but religion has a great deal to do with God. The distinction between the two perspectives is really very important for everyone to understand.

Separating issues regarding differences between the standard books included in *all* Bibles, versus those that are extra books as described in the last chapter, is also very important. This is the sort of separation problem that the atheist-myths implying that "the Bible is just a bunch of stories" are borne of. When we ourselves do not understand separations, such as the God-versus-religion issue just mentioned, it can cause us to unfairly project our often-incorrect religious views onto God, thus implying that God is responsible for our foolishness and incorrect conclusions, when in fact God is *not* responsible for *our* errors and misunderstanding.

When reading or studying the Bible, one of the most important mental separations for us to achieve is understanding the difference between the text or words as printed in the Bible, versus *our interpretation* of those words. To combat the basic problem of the difference between the text and our interpretation of that text, there are many who will strive to adhere to the *exact* wording of the text. But in doing so, they fail to grasp that the Bible has many versions that all have similar text, with each using a slightly different arrangement of words, but which all intend to convey the same general message or sentiment.

When we read and interpret the text *precisely* as it is written, we miss the implied messages and nature of the text. This is sort of like if someone calls your name and asks for you to come to help them and you say "I'll be there in a second." But will you really be there in one single second, or might it be five or ten seconds and maybe more? When we read words in a sentence, we typically understand that sentence to mean something different than the words alone might indicate. Written word carries with it intent and explanation that is conveyed in both smaller and larger concepts within it, and it is those concepts that we understand and convey with our words.

In knowing how to separate issues, we can more readily see the concepts intended within the text, but the real challenge comes in us sticking to the intended concepts and not unintentionally adding to them in our mind. The Bible is quite literal in its meanings in many parts of it, yet our human Earth-centric perspective clouds our understanding. For instance, understanding the separation issue regarding the words used versus the concepts that those words are conveying is a requirement when trying to understand Genesis chapter one as is discussed in *The Science of God – The First Four Days*.

Another key issue of separation is to understand that the various Bible versions are all quite harmonious, yet they have differences. One of those differences is in some of the names of the books in the Bible, and yet another difference is the various versions of the Bible.

Separate the Issues of God, The Bible, and Religion

One of our most prominent stumbling-blocks that few people seem to ever recognize is that there are mental separations to be made between *Religion* and *The Bible* and *God*. These three aspects are often used in sort of a synonymous manner in that they are all typically grouped as some sort of inseparable set. But be assured that *God* is *God* and is **not** the *Bible* or *religion*. Some might reject the notion that God is not the Bible because the Bible is often Referred to as "The Word of God". But while the Bible is a great book filled with words *from* God, us calling it the "The Word of God" cannot be correct, because, as a technicality, *Jesus The Christ* is claimed to be "The Word of God" made flesh.

The Bible tells of Jesus and how and why he came, but he is not the Bible. The Bible should be held in reverence and should be cherished and protected from being corrupted through bad translation, but it is **not** specifically "The Word of God". And the Bible is not religion, and religion is not the Bible. These are all separate and we must keep them mentally separated in our thinking.

Knowing that they are separate is important because then when you try to understand how and why they relate, you will have a far better view and understanding of the overall topic you are studying. Too often they are blindly clumped in a sort of mental ad-hoc manner, where people then end up blaming God for the foolish human translation errors in the Bible, or a good translation of the Bible gets blamed for our erred religious interpretations of it upon which we build our often-erred beliefs.

Keep these separate in your mind and do not blame the Bible or God for our human errors of interpretation. And do not blame God for Biblical errors that are almost certain to be caused by the fault of past translators. There are ways to find our path through these potential errors, and us knowing the distinctions just mentioned is our key to being able to do so.

Book Name Differences

If you were brought up in a Christian environment, then you are likely familiar with particular pronunciations and spellings of various books that are in the Bible. But when we begin to study the Bible and find out that there are additional books, it gets confusing because, aside of the additional books, many of the standard books in the Bible have somewhat different names or spellings than we might be familiar with depending upon which Bible version we are looking at. Yet, the text in the various Bibles is generally the same.

Let's say you have a Douay Rheims version of the Bible and you happen to come upon some preacher quoting from *1 Kings* or *1 Samuel*, then it's good to understand that there is a need for mental separation in this case, because finding *1 Samuel* in a Douay Rheims version is tricky due to the name differences. And looking at *1 Kings* would not make sense in connection with what the preacher is talking about because you would need to actually look in *3 Kings* in a Douay Rheims Bible to find the same text.

Below is a partial list of some of the book-name differences between some versions. The Vulgate column has more obvious differences due to it being in Latin. But the differences between the English Douay Rheims versus the King James versions gives you a pretty good idea that such differences exist. The text in each version is the same in each row in the following list:

Douay Rheims	King James	Vulgate
1 Kings	1 Samuel	1 Samuelis
2 Kings	2 Samuel	2 Samuelis
3 Kings	1 Kings	1 Regum
4 Kings	2 Kings	2 Regum

1 Paralipomenon	1 Chronicles	1 Paralipomenon
2 Paralipomenon	2 Chronicles	2 Paralipomenon
Canticle of Canticles	Song of Solomon	Canticum Canticorum
Jeremiae	Jeremiah	Jeremias
Aggaei	Haggai	Aggaeus
Sophoniae	Zephaniah	Sophonias

There are various Bible versions that might have slightly altered spellings of books names. Different languages obviously will have differences, but so will English translations that are derived from those languages. Realizing that these differences exist will assist you a great deal when trying to get to the root meaning of a particular verse you might be reading that you want some additional clarification on as you compare it to other versions.

Separating all the Versions of the Bible

Mentally separating issues surrounding the Bible is a bit more of a task when we begin to look into all of the different versions of the Bible that are available today. And it is at this point that a great deal of debate and conflict can arise as to which is the ultimate version of authority, or which version we should be reading.

There certainly are a lot of Bible Versions today, but that should never cause any of us to doubt the Bible's consistency as it was carried through the years. We often ask "If there are so many versions, then how can it be accurate?" We'll dig into the stacks of Bibles in another chapter. But for now, what we need to be able to keep separate in mind is that while there are many translations, the actual translations trail leading to a Bible we read today is typically very short, with only two or three versions between the oldest up until yours today.

So, this is what we need to remember most and keep separate in our heads: While a *translation* is in fact a *version,* a version is not always a full translation. There are many versions of the Bible available today, and there are many translations because the Bible is translated into nearly every language on Earth. But the translations to get from the oldest available material to what we have today is really very short, and those translations only occurred for the purpose of having the Bible be available in a specific language. So, depending upon which language a person speaks, the translation trail can be slightly different.

While the modern version you choose can most definitely affect your understanding of the text, it really all depends upon what you want to get out of the Bible. If you're just reading for basic information or for the Salvation message, then any Christian Bible will typically suffice, even a Children's Bible. But if you perhaps want to understand the scientific aspects of the Creation account in Genesis One so that you can discuss it intelligibly with people, then some versions will *not* be acceptable if you truly want to understand the Creation account and whether or not it is accurate. The Creation account is discussed in the first four volumes of *The Science of God,* and those volumes are split between the various scientific fields that commonly oppose the Creation account, such as astrophysics, microbiology, evolution etc. The Creation account requires an open mind and *several* open Bibles to arrive at a rational perspective along with some basic scientific knowledge. Later we'll get into why we sometimes need several Bibles open when we study.

As you can see, the Bible texts and their meanings have a lot of nuances to consider. These nuances are mostly due to our modern interpretations of the various Bible versions and our ability to be able to recognize and *mentally separate* the various issues that arise when reading the Bible. But, while it is helpful to realize that there are differences from one Bible version to another Bible version, us knowing more about the path that was taken to arrive at a few key versions is critical when doing any level of study using the Bible.

Chapter 8

Keys to Your Biblical Box

Versions, versions, versions! How did they all come about? If the Bible is a history of a people, then why isn't that history unambiguous or even perfectly identical in *every* version of the Bible?

The Bible is said to be a history of "God's people" explaining things from the beginning of the Creation of all things and then follows the rocky history of "God's people" all the way through to the promised Salvation through The Christ. This shouldn't be too difficult a task, right? Just record the basics and keep the history safely locked away.

If there is one thing that the Bible has clearly documented, it is the folly of mankind. If we are to believe the accounts listed in the Bible, then it is the folly of man that got Adam and Eve ousted from the Garden of Eden. It is the folly of man that angered God so intensely that God found it necessary to flood the entire globe and erase all but a few. And not long after the flood it is once again the folly of mankind who quickly turned to corruption and worshipping idols.

Once God chose his people, it wasn't long until those faithful chosen people fell into folly and angered God by no longer being faithful. This was to a point where the Godly-protection they once benefited from was no longer upon them. When God abandoned them due to their horrid behavior and unfaithful ways, that lack of protection allowed for them to be taken captive by invading armies. After many years in captivity, these people eventually dispersed and altogether lost their identities, with the exception of a small fragment of "Jews".

Now, with the very brief list of human failures just mentioned, think again as to why it might be a bit of a challenge to maintain the historical documentation during such upheaval. The list given in the previous paragraph is only the *major* failures, there are many more human failures detailed in the Bible that are not as extreme, but are still quite disruptive to a people. And yet, somehow these written accounts made their way through thousands of years of history and are shared around the globe unlike anything else ever before or since. It was incumbent upon God's "chosen people" to spread the truths about the Greatness of God and the Salvation God prepared for all people, and that is why we have Bibles today!

Who Cares About "God's People"?

Who cares about the Bible anyway? I mean after all, the Bible is said to be the history of "God's people", a people who are thought to be the Jews. So then, who cares about any of it if it's just for them? You do. And we all should. Why should we care?

The Bible is a very long book, and it certainly does follow a specific blood-line of people. But what we fail to understand is that Adam and Eve, who are mentioned in Genesis, are not the first parents of "God's people", they are the first parents of *all people* and if the Bible is to be believed, then that includes *you*. Here is a good place to apply the mental separations discussed in the last chapter.

Make a mental note that the people referred to as "God's people" were claimed by God at some point, but prior to that point there was no "God's people" distinction to be made, there was only those who knew God and those who did not.

While God's People are named at a point quite early in the Bible, we must also realize that anything before that applies to **all** people. And further, God's people interacted with many people who were not specifically claimed as "God's people". This means that the Bible touches many nations, in fact it touches all nations, and that is why it matters to *everyone* on earth, excepting none.

Sure, there are parts of the Bible that are somewhat irrelevant to various nations, but those parts are really very few. The "Israelites" are "God's people" and they were tasked with teaching all of the peoples of the world about the goodness of God and, ultimately, about Salvation. This education about the Bible is needed as is made evident by how often and how quickly humanity diverts to idolatry and utter immorality.

Even if someone is Jewish and they reject the idea that this "Jesus" person is the promised Savior, the Jews are still a part God's people and are thus still tasked with teaching the world about Salvation. But from a Jewish perspective, humanity is still waiting for that Salvation, where Christians, on the other hand, believe it to be found in the Son of Man who is Jesus The Christ.

Why Do I Need Salvation?

It was not my intention to mention anything about Salvation in this book, but since this book is about the Bible and its origins and construction *and its relevance to **all** people*, the topic cannot be ignored. This is because Salvation is what the human account begins and ends with in the Bible. This book, *Understanding The Bible*, is intended to offer you clarification on some aspects of the Bible that all too often cause us to get confused or altogether blinded when reading it.

Often, when we hear about Salvation, we ask, "Why do *I* need to be saved?–I'm a good person." Preachers will then go on to list all of the reasons that we're all sinners. But while our sins are no doubt very many, this is really *not* why we need Salvation. Yes, we humans in our depravity with our murders and cheating and stealing and lying and and and... have sinned–a lot! However, even if you do not do any sin and are perfect, you still cannot be "Saved". Why is this?

First it needs to be pointed out that if you're old enough to read this book, then it is very likely that you *have* sinned, thus you are probably *not* perfect or sinless. But what about a new born baby? What have they done? They could not yet have sinned since they have only been born a few moments. So, some people who die must then be sinless if they die as a newborn baby, right? Yes and no.

This whole Salvation subject really detracts from the point of this book, but it is truly important to know a little bit about it in order for you to understand specifically *why* the Bible matters to **all** humans who have ever lived and who ever *will* live here on our planet Earth.

Salvation begins in the Garden of Eden very early in Genesis. In fact, it is in chapter three where we humans make our first folly. Only three short pages into the entire Bible, we humans already blew it. As the story goes, the first Man and Woman, (Adam and Eve), were placed in Paradise when the "Serpent" came and lured them into its control, at which point they were then subservient to the Serpent. At that point God was very angry with them for following the advice of the Serpent and barred Adam and Eve from the Garden of Eden–no longer were they then allowed into that Paradise.

When Adam and Eve submitted themselves to the Serpent they were destined to spend eternity apart from God. They were in some manner genetically changed and could no longer be in the presence of God in that same way as they had been, and so this "genetic defect" was then passed to all of their offspring— That's us, *all* of us! This means that no descendants of Adam and Eve could ever again be with God in that way due to this defect that all humankind on Earth would inherit, regardless of anyone's purity. Is it fair that innocent babies should then spend eternity away from God, in Hell, for simply having been born?

Since God created mankind in the likeness of God, it was not good that we would never again be able to be with God in the same way as Adam and Eve were in the Garden. So in mercy and grace, God promised Adam and Eve that at some point in time, God would send *God's Word* to come and save them through a righteous offspring of Adam and Eve. In other words, at some point in time, a sinless descendent of Adam and Eve would be borne into this world and somehow save Adam and Eve and their righteous descendants so that mankind could once again return to God and be with God as Adam and Eve once were before they followed the advice of the Serpent.

It is quite common to hear the phrase "Jesus came to save us from our sins." which seems to imply that we have all sinned and need saving. But did Jesus really come to save us from our petty sins? No, that is not the reason that Jesus did the whole Crucifixion deal, and Died and allegedly went to Hell and then Rose from the Dead and eventually Ascended to Heaven.

The man we call Jesus is believed by Christians to be the promised sinless descendent of Adam and Eve, and Jesus came to save *all* of mankind from the grasp of Hell. Christ's arrival was not for the Jews, his arrival is for *anyone who ever lived on this Earth*. And something about his dying and having to go to Hell and then rising from the dead allows mankind the option of Salvation that *did not exist* prior to Christ's Resurrection. This is why even babies would have been separated from God and have been committed to Hell. However, since the Savior came, *all* humans *have the option of <u>choosing</u>* Salvation. This information can be easily obtained when reading any Christian Bible.

You might wonder how a baby would get to choose since they may have died before being offered a choice. But, we must again look at the reason behind Salvation and realize that it is highly unlikely that a God who created Salvation would not have a way for innocent babies who died to be able to make that choice. So, if you look at it in this light it might help a bit: Imagine a crawling baby who is in a completely dark room where there are two doors. Both doors are open, one is pitch black inside and filled with darkness, and from the other door shines a brilliant light. Now, which door do we imagine that a baby would crawl through? The baby is going to crawl through the only door that they can see. The baby will crawl to the Light! And even if they cannot yet crawl, and let's say that they were killed through abortion, if the baby had eyes, those eyes would turn to the *lighted* doorway rather than to the darkness if put in the same dark room as the crawling infant.

It is critical to understand that Salvation is not for Christians or for Jews or for Muslims. Salvation is **for _all_ of mankind** on Earth, and the Bible is the Testament to that Salvation. And *that* is why the Bible is for, and pertains to, __every__ person on Earth.

In our us-against-them-world, Christians have done a wonderful job spreading the "Good News" around the world, but too many people, many Christians included, believe that people of other religions cannot be saved. This gives the impression that Salvation is not for the people of these other religions, but this is simply not true. Salvation is offered to **all people on Earth**. And they have access to Salvation through reading the Bible and then following the instructions given by Jesus The Christ. People can have access to Salvation by just hearing about it and then following the simple instructions. There is no debating this point Biblically. Provided that people follow those instructions, Salvation can be theirs by accepting Jesus Christ as the Savior and sinning no more.

Understanding the point behind Salvation and why we all need it brings relevance to all people as to the purpose of the

Bible, and it is one of the Keys to opening your Biblical Box of understanding. Yet, even if we understand the basic premise of Salvation in the Bible, we still experience confusion in many areas of life when it comes to the Bible, such as the issues and questions surrounding Creation that the various volumes of the *The Science Of God* books guide readers through. At the center of that topic and the confusion within it, is the discussion surrounding Bible Versions and which are best for study.

Clearing some Confusion About Bible Versions

It is a certainty that a large number of people who read the book you are now reading will enter reading it with having believed or been told "the Bible is probably not reliable because it has been translated so many times that it must be all messed up *if* it's even true to begin with". And if it's not the case that we believe or were told that today, it still likely was the case at some point in our past, or we will hear it in our future.

The *Bible versions* topic is a huge topic and a point of contention between believers and non-believers alike, and truth be told, neither group has much of a grasp on any of it. There certainly are those who are familiar with the translations trail, but they are few in number.

People who are new to researching the Bible are often told that the Bible has been translated and retranslated so many times that it simply cannot be trusted. This is both true and false. It is true because the Bible has been translated into nearly every language on Earth, and often it is translated from a version that has already been translated from another language. However, the idea of an endless translation trail is false. The tree of translations is really quite small. It starts with a trunk of original material, which as far as most scholars suspect is no longer available and would likely have been written in an ancient Hebrew script that is very different from the modern Hebrew script that we see today.

Since the originals are either hidden or lost, the best we can do is to revert to the oldest known copies, and this is where the topic gets a bit complicated. If you have ever heard the story or watched a movie about the "Ten Commandments", or if you actually read the account in the Bible, then you may have recalled that some of the Bible books that were written back then were kept in the "Ark of the Covenant", (not Noah's ark, that's a large boat. The Ark of the Covenant is a much smaller gold-clad box that God's people kept important items in for safe keeping.) These are the first several books of the Bible. And it is these books that have been the most protected and prolifically transcribed over the centuries. They are often referred to as the "Torah", which means to *teach*.

After these books where placed into the Ark and the Israelites had gone through their forty-year desert journey, they began to continue to record their history as it occurred. Similar to what we did in recent times before the age of electronics—*they wrote it down by hand*. The Israelites even recorded the not-so-flattering aspects of their history. As their history built, it was kept each in its own history and writings set which became a categorization of topics or event era, some of those writings sets were occurring simultaneously.

There are many things detailed in the Bible that were occurring in unison during the same time period, making it sometimes hard to follow. But, *you knowing* that this is the case will help you a great deal in seeing through the fog of confusion that we typically have when trying to understand the wealth of information that we read in the Bible. While the Books of the Bible are generally arranged in chronological order, events detailed in one book may have been occurring at the same time that events detailed in another book were occurring, this is because some of the Old Testament books are parallel information. This means that two parallel events were occurring at the same time, often in reference to each other, but each was being recorded from a different perspective in a different region by different people. Keep that clearly in mind, because if you do not remember that, then the Bible will be far more confusing when reading it.

Before we get any further into the *Bible versions* subject, you must understand that it is *not* a brief topic. Volumes of books have been written on this very subject. So here in this book, we're not going to dwell on the many deeper details of the hundreds of translations. Instead, the goal is to have everyone understand the basic and quite *short* path that the Bible took to get here as we see it today. And this is perhaps your most critical required key to open your Biblical box of understanding, thus enabling your box of understanding to overflow.

The Basic Biblical Translations Path

The Bible is not a single book passed down for thousands of years. It was a recording of events and writings of the time and were added to as time progressed, but the bulk of the additions ended when the Israelites lost their identity. After that, the additions were few, until the arrival of Jesus The Christ, who the Jews do *not* recognize as The Savior Christ. While the documentation trail actually starts at the beginning of Creation, what we are concerned with are the actual translations.

When God's people were dispersed they carried with them their documented history and eventually that history was meticulously copied for the tribes of Israel. So, the term "originals" in the context of Bible study would be any of the original copies in the native language of the people. The tribes would have carried those copies with them. Since the existing Hebrew documents are not dated with copyright dates as books are today, we really don't have confirmation that some ancient Hebrew texts found today are specifically part of those original copies. So, starting with the oldest copies that are still existent today, the following are the translation descendants of those texts and the approximate year each entered the scene:

1. 1450 BC through 285 BC The Original Ancient Hebrew as written, along with any copies for each tribe.

2. 285 BC The Greek Septuagint

3. 0 AD through 150 AD Added The Greek New Testament

4. 382 AD The Latin Vulgate

5. 1522 AD through 1609 AD The King James Bible, The Guttenberg Bible, The Douay Rheims, and The German Luther Bible

Translations Descendancy

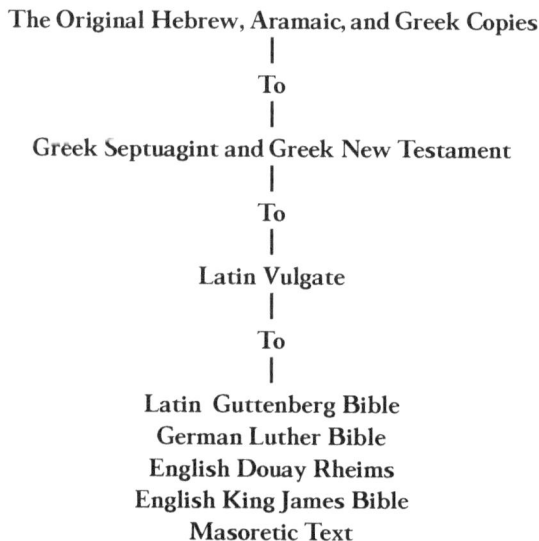

The Original Hebrew, Aramaic, and Greek Copies
|
To
|
Greek Septuagint and Greek New Testament
|
To
|
Latin Vulgate
|
To
|
Latin Guttenberg Bible
German Luther Bible
English Douay Rheims
English King James Bible
Masoretic Text

The beauty of this short tree of translation descendancy is that besides some of the Original Hebrew copies being no longer available, it is generally all still in existence today for us to revert back to in order to confirm accuracy and for study. And facsimiles of these are digitally available to you today. I highly recommend that everyone try to find and download copies of them as soon as possible. And if you're really into Biblical study, you can even go as far as printing out a copy of each for you own reference, or you can buy printed copies of these versions of antiquity that match your study needs.

Chapter 9

Embracing All Those Versions

The fact that the Bible has so many versions and has been translated so many times is thought to be its biggest flaw. But is it really a flaw? Are multiple translations really a bad thing?

Sure, it would be great to have all of the "*original*" writings that compose the Bible, but since that is unlikely to happen anytime soon, we must work with what we have. And that is where we change from the vast number of versions being the Bible's biggest flaw, to it being the Bible's biggest blessing! We must embrace this vast collection of versions and be thankful for it, and in this chapter you'll find out why.

The *Translations Descendancy list* or *translation trail* from the last chapter is short—very short considering the timespan involved. And since there are copies of the texts in that trail that are still in existence today, the trail is even shorter because we can still go back to an actual printed copy of any version that is on that trail.

Beginning the Bible

We discussed the word "Bible" and the fact that it comes from a city named *Byblos*. And we discussed the need for casting away our opaque-black- and rose-colored agenda-driven glasses before reading or studying the Bible. We dove into our need for mental separations and how the need for Salvation came about. We even visited the subject of the Bible's supposed "inerrancy" which we now get to do a bit of hair-splitting on to see if the Bible could remain inerrant through so many translations, or if it even matters. So, just why are there so many different versions and translations of the Bible? While the Translations Descendancy list is actually very short, there were some predecessors to the versions on the bottom of that list.

The first notable assembly of "Biblical" text is the Greek "Septuagint" which dated to the second century BC, or close to 300 years **before** the Crucifixion and Resurrection of The Christ. This then would obviously not have included the New Testament texts since those events had not yet occurred at that time. The *New Testament* is the History of events beginning at the birth of Christ. The *Old Testament* is the entire span of history of the people *before* the birth of Christ.

The Original Hebrew Copies

As the people, referred to as "God's People", or the Israelites, recorded events and compiled their history over a period of roughly two thousand years, each of the twelve tribes had copies of the information. But much the way families with multiple generations begin to have differing history along each new branch of the family tree, so too did the tribes of the Israelites. The key events of these tribes where eventually combined into the single work we refer to as the "Hebrew Bible" or the "Old Testament". And this is what was translated and is referred to as the Greek "Septuagint".

The Greek Septuagint Translation

The name "Septuagint" comes from the Greek word "septuāgintā" meaning *seventy*, which is named so because, as the account goes, seventy-two Jewish scholars worked to translate the original Hebrew copies into the Greek language.

A group of scholars, six from each of the twelve tribes of Israel, independently translated the text from its native language into Greek, and each of the twelve translations were said to be identical. This was a form of checking for accuracy. Now, in our fantasy Christian view, we can believe that when this took place that the versions were perfectly identical, but while they were likely very accurate, do not assume that they were like the photocopies that we make today.

Remember here, that they were translating this text and they were doing so as accurately as they possibly could. This leaves little room for error if those who are doing the translating are being truthful in trying to convey the intent of the original language into the newly translated language.

After the Israelites were taken captive and taken out of the land of Israel around six-hundred years before Christ, those from the tribe of Judah still were able to remain in Jerusalem. But eventually they too were taken captive and taken away from the land of Israel. Then after several decades, they were able to return to Jerusalem.

After several centuries, some of these "Jewish" scholars were asked to translate the books that had eventually been gathered at the library in Alexandria, Egypt. The scholars were instructed to take the books that describe the events of history and to translate those books into the Greek language—and that translation is what we call the "Septuagint".

How do we know these things? The historian Josephus tells of a letter that described a request by the library at Alexandria, Egypt, for a Greek translation to be compiled by seventy-two interpreters who were sent to Alexandria from Jerusalem. This newly compiled translation is what we today refer to as the "Septuagint".

The Septuagint stood the test of time for around six centuries when it was then compiled together with the other newer mostly Greek and Latin writings that comprise the New Testament. This new compilation of the Septuagint and the New Testament documents were then translated into Latin and is, today, referred to as the "Latin Vulgate".

The Vulgate Translation

It is important to understand the timeframes involved here. The Latin Vulgate was commissioned to be compiled and translated by Jerome, beginning roughly 382 years *after* the birth of Christ, and it took about fifteen years to complete.

The start of the Jerome Vulgate translation was only about 350 years after The Christ was said to have risen from the dead. We must compare this to the history of the United States in that the history was still quite comparatively fresh at the time of Jerome, versus overall history.

Further, the time between the resurrection and the assembly of the Vulgate was a time of prolific spread of Christianity. And in their effort to share this information, copies of the Gospels where made, and also were shared from memory. In these translations there were misunderstandings or even errors that some epistles themselves mention in the actual texts that caution the people to not be deceived by inaccurate accounts about Christ, or letters falsely claiming to be from some of those writers.

So, around 325 years after the birth of Christ or only about 290 years after the Resurrection of Christ, the bishops of the various regions convened a council at Nicaea, Greece, as requested by the Roman Emperor Constantine I. The council was convened as an effort to establish the consensus on issues surrounding the Church, part of which was to determine which Biblical information was accurate and to root out proliferation of erroneous accounts of Christ and the Epistles. Many more bishops are said to have been invited, but only around 300 where able to attend. It is these 300 Bishops that collectively decided on which books and which versions of them would become the official canon, which is now what we read today as "the Bible".

We'll get into this a bit more, but understanding that there are basically only two translations up to this point speaks for the very short translation descendancy list of the Bible. Of these two translations, the *Septuagint* and the *Vulgate*, the Septuagint was the primary text for about six hundred years and it is still used to this day.

There were Latin translations before the assembly of the Jerome Vulgate, but they had known errors in them which is partly why the council at Nicaea was convened. After the Septuagint and some other older Hebrew texts were eventually translated into Latin, the Latin Vulgate became the standard for about twelve hundred years up to around the time of the Reformation in the early 1500s.

This is where it begins to get a bit cloudy and the various versions come on the scene. The Jerome Vulgate was revised for clarity around 1590 AD to clean up margin notes in Jerome's work, this revision is known as the Sixto-Clementine Vulgate. But other versions were already in the works.

So Many Versions

How many Bible version are there really? Not as many as it appears. While the Bible does have a translation for nearly every language on Earth today, most of those translations are translated from one of a small selection of Bible translations and versions.

If you recall, earlier it was pointed out that there is a distinction to be made between *translations* and *versions*. A translation is a version, but a version is not always a translation. A "translation" has the purpose of changing text from one language to another so that it can be readily read and understood by people who speak the language of the newly translated text.

We can get particular and claim that some of the newer Bibles that attempt to make the text more readable by modernizing it, are technically "translations", but while that claim has some legitimacy, it is not really correct. Changing the words of a Bible from English to English for clarification purposes is actually more of revision, which clearly places it into a *version* category. Where *translating* is changing the native tongue or language of the text, which up until the Reformation only occurred twice in the translation tree in nearly two thousand years with the Septuagint and the Vulgate.

Latin Gutenberg Vulgate Bible

Before discussing the Gutenberg Bible, we must discuss the Gutenberg Printing Press. There is much misunderstanding regarding the idea of printing that few people care about or realize. Mass duplication of pages has been done since around the second century AD in the form of woodblock printing. Woodblock printing is a single wooden plate that has all of the words carved backwards so that when it is covered with ink and pressed onto a paper it will produce exact duplications of a single page of text. Some early Bibles used this method of duplication rather than the tedious and error prone task of word by word hand transcription one letter and one word at a time. This revolution in duplication was not widely available until about eight-hundred years later when moveable-type entered the scene during the mid-eleventh century.

Moveable type was a revolution because only a given number of each word needed to be carved and then could be rearranged for each consecutive page of the Bible being printed. This is as opposed to a uniquely carved one-piece plate for each page of the Bible.

This allowed for many pages to be printed in a single day. However, due to the steps involved in hand-laid impressions, this method allowed for easy smearing of any piece of parchment as it was being pressed and removed, causing the entire procedure to be a slow and very tedious process in effort to avoid waste.

Four-hundred years later, around 1440 AD, a man by the name of Johannes Gutenberg created a machine made of wood that could evenly and quickly press a sheet of paper against a plate of movable type covered with ink. This made duplication considerably faster and it made for a cleaner better copy on each paper printed. The Gutenberg Printing Press took the printing speeds from roughly fifty pages per day to several thousand pages per day. Speeding printing up from roughly fifty prints per day was an increase in speed of a factor of about 60 to 80 *times* more pages per day. This was a revolution in the proliferation of Bible distribution.

After Gutenberg's invention of the printing press, the first mass printed Bibles were printed on the press and completed sometime during the 1450s. This first edition was a version of the Latin Vulgate, some of which are still in existence to this day. These beautifully printed copies of the Latin Vulgate are one of the important bridges needed verify our Bibles of today.

Every different Bible version of antiquity that is still in existence is an important part of the bridge from the original Hebrew text copies to our Bibles of today. While the Gutenberg Latin Vulgate Bible was the beginning of the revolution of mass-printed Bibles, it was certainly not the end. That revolution continues to this very day. The Gutenberg Bible is little different than the Jerome Vulgate. The Gutenberg Bibles were essentially merely copies of Jerome's Vulgate Bible assembly and they are copies that are frozen in time dating to about 1450 AD. When we look back at a copy of a Gutenberg Bible, we are looking back, first-hand, at the Bible as it was well more than a half millennium ago. The Gutenberg Bible was printed roughly seventy years *before* the Reformation era began when most Bibles in existence at that time had been produced in the Latin language at a time when all Christians were essentially "Catholic". Many Christians, by definition, are still "Catholic" today but do not realize that fact. See the book *Understanding The Church* for more on that subject.

Translation Versions

Each of us needs to inquire about these things within our own mind and eventually make some decisions about what we conclude and thus what we will believe about the Bible's text and its accuracy. Doing so is far easier when we clear the confusion about the earlier translations. Knowing that only two language to language translations occurred between the original Hebrew text copies and the text of nearly two thousand years later, helps us a great deal, but what about all of the translations that came later out of the Reformation era?

The main Bible Versions of the Reformation era are, in general, derived from the Original Hebrew text copies, and the Greek Septuagint along with the mostly Greek texts of the New Testament and the Latin Vulgate. These newer Reformation era Bible Versions are abundant.

Before the Reformation, regarding Christianity and Israel, there wasn't really a religious distinction other than between Jew and Christian and Pagan. And since we are discussing the Bible's formation, only the Jews and Christians are a part of the discussion here. This means that everyone in the discussion was a Christian if they were not Jewish. We can state this in modern terms that everyone was Catholic at that time if they were not Jewish since the seat of the Church was Rome and "Catholic" means universal, and the Reformation had not yet occurred.

Around the ninth century, the Catholic Church leaders began to offer a path to Salvation through the offering of "indulgences". *Indulgences* were initially prescribed to people to make up for their own sins as a form of repentance and penance. Our *Indulgences* that we did could then be credited to loved ones who had already died. Indulgences had been practiced as a means of removal of punishment for sin and had been implemented for several centuries before the idea of exchanging money as a form of indulgence occurred.

Eventually, in effort to build Saint Peters Basilica in Rome, Italy, Church leaders began a fund-raising effort for the cathedral through selling indulgences. But as humanity goes, the sale of indulgences not only funded the building of Saint Peter's Basilica, it also enriched a small handful of greedy church leaders across the land. This obvious abuse was not taken well by people in the various regions.

As you can likely understand, at no time in our history have we humans not been in contention with our neighbor. As the Christian Church spread, the regional differences arose regarding church control of the various regions. The Seat of the Church was Rome and the Head of the Church was the Pope. In 1517 Pope Leo X made the declaration that those who contributed to the construction of Saint Peters Basilica cathedral would be granted indulgence. Money in exchange for remission of sins had now been officially declared by the Pope, and it was a step too far for many people. As the pressures mounted for the church-body to purchase indulgences, the citizens and leaders of the churches from various regions began pushing back against this abuse and misapplication of indulgences.

In the early 1500s, a man named Martin Luther was a Catholic priest who became frustrated by the Pope's declaration about a financial exchange for indulgences. It is said that as an act of rebellion against clergy selling indulgences, Martin Luther nailed to the door of All Saints' Church and other churches in Wittenberg, his Ninety-Five Theses.

Luther's Ninety-Five Theses listed ninety-five points why Salvation cannot be purchased with money and that it is by faith alone that Salvation is obtained. Luther's complaint was largely ineffective for about four years until 1521 AD at the "Edict of Worms". The assembly at the city of Worms was an imperial assembly of the Holy Roman Empire called by Emperor Charles V, held at the Heylshof Garden in Worms, Germany from which the Edict of Worms arose. The edict prohibited citizens of the Holy Roman Empire from spreading Luther's Ninety-Five Theses.

This edict ignited the pent-up animosity that had been building for several years regarding the exchange of money for indulgences, along with some other issues of regional control and other doctrinal principles. The posting of the Ninety-Five Theses and the Edict of Worms, together, began the Reformation era which lasted for about one-hundred-thirty years.

German Language - Luther Bible

After posting his Ninety-Five Theses, Martin Luther was sequestered in the Wartburg Castle when he began to translate the New Testament from Greek into German in order to make it more accessible to German-speaking people of the Holy Roman Empire. Using a Greek 1519 second-edition prepared by the Dutch priest/philosopher/scholar Erasmus, Luther translated the entire New Testament into German. Following this, Luther worked with several others to complete the translation of the entire Bible into German, which was completed in 1534. This is believed to be the first ever German Language Bible.

Because of the relatively recent invention of the Gutenberg printing press, by the time the German-language-Luther-Bible was composed and ready, it was easily duplicated in mass quantity and therefore was able to be distributed to the people in record time.

English Language - The Great Bible To King James

Coincidentally, around the same time that the German Bible was completed, all churches in England were still under the jurisdiction of Rome. But people from many areas outside of Rome had become frustrated with the sale of indulgences and other issues arising between Rome and some churches in other regions. In 1534 The King of England, King Henry VIII, wanted a male heir, but his wife Catherine of Aragon did not produce any sons, so King Henry VIII requested an annulment that he wanted to be given by the church for his marriage to Catherine. But the Papacy refused to grant the annulment. The Pope's rejection of Henry's annulment request angered King Henry VIII, causing him to renounce Papal authority, resulting in the formation of the church of England.

By 1539 the first English language edition of the Bible was produced and was authorized by King Henry VIII. But the production of this version was difficult in coming. Henry promised this new English Bible would be translated by Catholic scholars, but he must have met with resistance since he rejected the papacy of Rome. An attempt was also made to have some of the English bishops collaborate to translate the New Testament into English, but they failed to deliver in a timely manner. The entire process was wrought with problems, and finding capable and dedicated translators in England was difficult at that time. The first known *complete* English language version of the Bible, referred to as *The Great Bible,* was compiled in an ad-hoc manner using various sources, some of which were authoritative and some not. But this was progress, and it allowed English speaking people to finally hear the Bible read to them in their own tongue.

After the publication of the 1539 *Great Bible* in English, other people attempted to assemble and translate a better, more accurate, English Bible now known as the *Geneva Bible*. This effort began around 1557 and was completed around 1576. But as the various books were translated and made their rounds, it offended some leaders of the Church of England. King Henry VIII wanted *his* authorized version to be translated from the Hebrew, Aramaic, and Greek, but since he had difficulty procuring skilled translators capable of translation from those languages into English, much of the 1539 *Great Bible* ended up being translated from the Latin Vulgate.

To competitively combat the objectionable *Geneva Bible* that was produced in the English Language, the next major step in the evolution of King Henry's protestant English 1539 *Great Bible* was a new version referred to as the English *Bishop's Bible,* first published in 1568. These attempts were all to bypass the Latin Vulgate Bible as the primary source for translation in effort to have the source material for the Church of England's authorized Bible be the original Hebrew, Aramaic, Greek, and Latin texts. But all these efforts were left wanting.

The next major step in the Church of England's authorized English language Bible was the King James version. In this version additional effort was made to translate using Hebrew, Aramaic, Greek, and Latin which was finally accomplished. The authorized King James Bible was finally published in 1611. There is much more detail to the story occurring between the English Language Great Bible Version and the King James 1611 Version, but here we only mentioned the key points, some of which are themselves difficult to document. Ultimately, the 1611 King James Bible is translated from the original Hebrew, Aramaic, Greek, and Latin texts, with guidance from existing English and Latin Bible versions of that time.

English Language - Douay Rheims Bible

The Douay Rheims Bible is an English Translation of the Latin Vulgate. The New Testament was translated in Reims France in 1582 and Old Testament was fully translated in the city Douai France at a Catholic Seminary and was completed in 1610.

While the Douay Rheims Bible has a fairly clear history, it too had revisions. The original Douay Rheims Bible text had been translated straight from Latin into English, but had used difficult to understand "Latinate" words, ultimately prompting it to be revised.

A revision of the Douay Rheims Bible was done by Bishop Challoner between 1749 and 1752 to make it more readable. This version was influenced by the King James version and by the Sixto-Clementine Version of Jerome's Vulgate.

Hebrew Language - Masoretic Text

The "Hebrew Bible" is a bit of a tough subject to try to grasp in one sitting. The term "Hebrew Bible" gives us an impression that the books of the Bible were already assembled and bound by the Hebrews or Israelites, but this is an incorrect thought. As mentioned in an early section, the Israelites would have had multiple copies of these histories for each tribe and it is from these copies that all other translations descend. But we tend to associate the "Hebrew Bible" solely with the Jews that came out of captivity with their newly adopted, what we call, "Modern Hebrew" script. The copies of the Biblical books that they carried eventually had been translated into this modern Hebrew text.

Between about 500 AD and 900 AD, groups of Jewish scholars developed a system of pronunciation markings to assist in standardizing pronunciation when reading text. This "Masorah" system means to fix in place, or in this case, to "make standard", and the scholars who created this system are called the Masoretes. Their version of the text is referred to as the Masoretic Text. The oldest know Masoretic text dates back only to about 900 AD.

Basic Summary

Should all of this translation-and-versions fog cause us to doubt the consistency of the Bible? No, it is quite the opposite. We, today, with all of our technology, have the ability to see actual copies of all of the finished various Bible versions and the ancient texts in all of their glory. But we also still have access to original copies of most items on the versions trail that leads to each of them. So, while adjustments were made for clarity in nearly every Bible translation ever made, each is done in full view of the world and alongside *all* other versions together with all versions leading to each subsequent version of the Bible. It is an unparalleled and very impressive cross-reference system with over two-thousand years of cross-checking and validation.

Chapter 10

Commit to Having an Open Biblical Box

The tiny mental boxes that many of us force our Bibles into cost us dearly regarding our own understanding of the Bible. When we are told that there are "just too many translations" in the translation trail leading to any one Bible, it is simply *not* true.

Each key version in Latin, English, and German all point back to the same Hebrew, Aramaic, and Greek texts. But if we imagine for a moment that the English and German language Bibles have not been influenced by the Jerome Vulgate, then we are sadly mistaken. The grievances against the Papacy came long after the Jerome Vulgate. As Germany and England did their best to break away from the Papacy in Rome, they were in fact a part of that church up until the Reformation era. This means that everyone was part of the Holy Roman Empire and thus by today's terminology, *all* were Catholics. At that time the entire church used the Latin Vulgate as its Authorized Bible. This Latin influence and understanding of the text, by the translators, was not erased from their preconceptions of the text.

The effort to step away from the Vulgate had a three-pronged purpose. The first was ultimately a rejection of the Papacy in Rome and to step away from the Latin language. But, the more important issue to them was to translate the Bible into the Native language of the German and English-speaking peoples so that the Mass and Bible reading could be done in their native languages.

So as to have a more pure translation, both the German and English languages worked to create pure translations from the same sources from which the Latin Vulgate had been translated. This would place these new German and English translations on a translation level equal to that of the Latin Vulgate. You'll quickly understand the need for this if you are reading or have read any of the *The Science of God* volumes.

Whenever we translate from one language to another, we tend to lose some of the nuances of the original language. Doing this several times from language to language can utterly diminish a text to a point of being nearly useless. This is why such extreme care and effort was put into each language translation. These early translations, the 382 Latin Vulgate Bible, the 1522 German Luther Bible, and the 1611 English King James Bible are all ultimately translated from the original copies of Hebrew, Aramaic, Greek, and Latin texts. This means that there is really only **one** language-to-language translation for many who read the Bible today. That is to say from Hebrew to English, and from Aramaic to English, and from Greek to English, and from Latin to English depending upon which parts of the Bible you are reading. And if it is not translated to English, then it is either translated to Latin or to German regarding these primary versions.

The Purpose of Revisions

Revisions of the Bible are many, and they tend to increase every handful of years. However, the revisions are typically done as a clarification or a modernizing of a term. Some of these revisions do in fact harm the text, but most of that injury is relegated to a few somewhat non-authoritative Bible versions.

When Bibles were printed in the 1500s and 1600s it was a considerably greater task than it is today. They didn't take it lightly and they wanted the text to be accurate. So changes would be made to adjust translated words that could be stated in a clearer manner. There are also issues of grammar. For instance, we can say something two very different ways but intend to mean the exact same thing.

Consider these two statements:

1. There are also issues of grammar.

2. Grammatical concerns also exist.

Both statements are acceptable, but sometimes the way something is stated can be confusing, and when those instances are brought to the attention of those who work on Biblical accuracy in reprints, they will then work to restate the text in question so as to remove potential confusion.

We can also use a different word when translating, where to the particular translator the word might be fine, yet someone who reads the translation will potentially see that same text slightly different than intended by the translator.

Consider these two statements:

1. You *must* visit them.

2. You *will* visit them.

Is there a difference? Some will say yes, and some will say no. But when challenged on the text, scholars will look back at the Hebrew, Aramaic, Greek, and Latin and see which term if either would be the best fit.

These are the types of reasons that revisions are made. Nearly every Bible translation and version that has ever been produced was produced for clarity. Imagine having to read a Bible printed in the German language if you are not able to read or speak German.

Now, realize that up until the 1960s, Catholic masses were said in Latin. This means that almost none of the English-speaking Catholic congregations in the United Stated could actually understand the Mass as it was taking place in Latin. The same was true of any other language people. Aside of it being a massive undertaking to translate the Bible in to any language, the most prominent reason that the church was ever-reluctant to change the language was loss of accuracy.

Those are a few reasons why the Bible has been translated and why it gets updated. Now imagine yourself not having a translation of the Bible that *you* are able to read and understand, and your only source of Biblical information was in Latin, but you can only read and understand English.

The Benefits of Versions

While the versions-and-translations confusion feels like a lost cause, it is not. These various versions and all of the infighting between the various Christian divisions is a blessing, and here's why: With the key language groups all competing against one another and them seeking the highest level of accuracy, we today are the beneficiaries of these accuracy efforts. Had this not been the case, then the only version today would be the original Latin Vulgate, which needed some work, and there would never have been anything to test the Latin Vulgate with, other than the original text copies.

The original text copies are certainly something good to compare to, but if the Bible was only ever seen through the eyes of the Latin Vulgate, then many people today would be unable to understand it because they do not know the Latin language. And those who could understand the language would only be able to interpret it through the Latin Vulgate lens.

When the German and English versions came onto the scene it began a new era of the Bible, bringing it to millions of people who prior to that time did not have access to the Bible other than through their churches and priests. The Gutenberg printing revolution, together with the German and English translation efforts, allowed for a whole new level of Biblical scrutiny.

While previous translation efforts were noble causes, and were likely well done by prepared scholars, both the Greek translation of the original texts that occurred before Christ, as well as the Latin Vulgate that occurred after Christ, still potentially would contain some of the grammatical issues mentioned in the last section. This does not make them wrong or in error, but it could make phrases in those versions confusing to some readers. And if the readers do not have the original text accessible to themselves, or if they do not know how to read the original Hebrew, then they are left only with their own interpretation of the translated version.

When we consider that we debate in the Supreme Court about the meaning and intentions embodied in the Constitution of the United States, which is written in a language we all know very well, then we have to realize the magnitude of the task of translating *any* text from another language. The text of the books in the Bible has been discussed and debated for *thousands* of years, and it is the various translations that allows some of these debates to occur.

These translations are not a stumbling block to us, they are a blessing to us! With all of the debate that has arisen between all of the Bible scholars about all of the versions through all of the Bible's history, we can be pretty sure that many of the Bible translation versions of today are acceptably translated.

Probably the most important point to realize about all of the translations is that it is not specifically this translation or that translation that is **the** one, but rather it is all of them together. When studying the Bible, we should not base every point we are attempting to clarify on a single version, we should be looking at the main language versions side by side in attempt to extract the nuances of the original Hebrew, Aramaic, Greek, and Latin text copies.

- Hebrew – 900 AD Masoretic Text

The main Bible versions that include the New Testament are:
- Latin – 382 AD Vulgate Bible

- German – 1522 AD Luther Bible

- English – 1582 AD Douay Rheims Bible

- English – 1611 AD King James Bible

Without the main Bible versions listed above, most of the Bibles we read today would simply not exist. And today we also have the luxury of technology that allows us to obtain actual digital photographic copies of these early versions so that we can see them first-hand. Adding to this, we now also, through technology, can obtain live text copies of these same versions of antiquity, allowing us to do text searches within them. These are study luxuries unparalleled in history, and there is no other text on earth that receives the same level of scrutiny as the Bible has for thousands of years *and* as the Bible still receives to this day. The only document that ever even came close is The Constitution of the United States of America.

The Bible will continue to be a debated set of documents for the foreseeable future, and the more scholars who debate and discuss its content the better it is for everyone. However, we must guard ourselves against the folly of fools, because there are those who have clever tongues with an agenda to drive us away from studying, or even just reading the Bible. Never trust anyone who tells you to *not* read the Bible. Every person should read it and be afforded the opportunity to decide for themselves what value the contents of the Bible has to them.

For those who pursue the study of the Bible, you would benefit from obtaining digital copies of the ultimate source material.

The original or oldest text copies are:

- Hebrew copies

- Aramaic copies

- Greek copies

- Latin Copies

Christians and non-Christians alike will continue the petty infighting about translation issues, but each new translation is largely in harmony. This is truly a gift and a wonderful testament to the key versions and the accuracy of their translation. The order of the translations shown in the Translation Descendancy Tree at the end of chapter eight illustrates the order that these translation versions occurred, but the actual translation tree is really more like the following:

The Original Hebrew, Aramaic, and Greek Copies

|

TO

|

All together:
Greek Septuagint
Latin Vulgate
Latin Guttenberg Bible
German Luther Bible
Douay Rheims
English King James Bible
Masoretic Text

While each version can claim its roots in the original copies, the truth is that is a combination of being rooted in the original copies alongside of the major predecessor. Meaning that, as a technicality, the only version that can legitimately claim to be solely taken from the original Hebrew, Aramaic, and Greek copies is the Greek Septuagint. All other translations that followed have been influenced in some manner by the Septuagint. And all translations that occurred after the Latin Vulgate have in some manner been influenced by the Greek Septuagint *and* the Latin Vulgate, even if they claim to have used only the original Hebrew, Aramaic, Latin, and Greek copies.

Regardless of the influence that any earlier version might have had upon a later version, the fundamental point to keep in mind is that they are all ultimately rooted in the original Hebrew, Aramaic, Greek, and Latin copies because their translation teams all sought to go back to the originals for the sake of accuracy.

Double Checking Accuracy Over the Years

These key versions of the Bible have been meticulously investigated and compared and critiqued by what are essentially competing forces ever since the Reformation era. The key versions just listed have been compared against each other and have proven to be adequately consistent to a point that all of them agree and are synchronous. Petty differences do exist, but those will likely be debated for years to come, and most of the differences that cause some debate are minor issues, which are typically pointed out by those who are trying to discredit the Bible. While it might seem annoying to us, it is really important that people keep these debates going whenever questions arise. This practice has been going on since the Septuagint and it will and must continue if we want to be able to consider the Bible accurately translated.

This competitive check system is very good, because if someone from one of the Christian divisions or from the Jews steps out of line on a change in one of their revisions, that change is certain to become the focus of much scrutiny and is sure to be removed in a future version if it cannot be substantiated. It is truly a beautiful system and a clear testament of the consistency with which the Bible has been translated. But have there been any other means to check the Bible's consistency over the years?

Qumran Scrolls

Several hundred years after the key translations prepared between 1522 and 1611 had been completed, a discovery was made in caves in Qumran which contained hundreds of scrolls that are believed to have been hiding in those caves since roughly only one-hundred-fifty years *after* the Resurrection of Christ.

Many of these scrolls are copies, or fragments of copies, of some of the books that we find in our Bibles today. This discovery was made in the mid 1900s, and is perhaps the most compelling evidence of the consistency between the Septuagint and the Bibles we read today.

Because the Latin Vulgate was translated *after* these scrolls were hidden in the caves at Qumran until 1947, this find is of particularly high value regarding verification of our modern Bibles. The original Hebrew, Aramaic, and Greek copies were translated into the Greek Septuagint in the third century *before* the birth of Jesus The Christ. Since the texts found in the Qumran caves were found in 1947 and are believed to predate the Latin Vulgate by roughly 200 years, it means that any Bibles assembled and translated between the Greek Septuagint and up until Bibles printed any time before 1947 could *not* have been influenced by the Qumran texts.

The Qumran Caves texts have been frozen in time for nearly two millenia. This has two critical factors. The first is that people from nearly two thousand years ago thought that these texts were important enough that they should be protected by sealing and hiding them because these texts meant something special to those who hid them. The second factor is that these texts could not have influenced any of our modern Bibles up until 1947, nor could our Bibles have influenced those texts, making them a perfect check system to use to test the translation consistency of our modern Bibles.

The Qumran texts sat quietly hidden through the Latin Vulgate and through the Gutenberg Bible and through the translations of the German Luther Bible, the English Douay Rheims Bible, and the English King James Bible, and they further sat in wait through the many new versions that began to proliferate in the 1800s when the motorized mechanization of the printing press began.

Through all of this, the Bible has maintained its integrity as a document able to carry forward its information and then finally to have parts of the Bible compared to the Qumran text copies that have been archived for over eighteen-hundred years and finding little difference.

But this Proves Nothing

It is clearly established that the Bible has been meticulously translated into several key languages, and that competing Christian divisions, as well as Jewish scholars, have been scrutinizing each other's Bible versions and critiquing them for a very long time, thus forcing Biblical translation accuracy. But this proves nothing about the Bible other than it has been reasonably accurately translated for thousands of years. If you look into this with any bit of integrity, you would be a fool to deny that Bibles are, in general, very *accurately translated*. But the real question is, are they accurate? This is connected with the question asked early in this book as to whether or not the Bible is true.

This is one of those mental separation areas spoken of earlier that we all need to have clearly established in our mind. The Bible being translated accurately is really quite irrelevant if you happen to be looking at the original Hebrew, Aramaic, and Greek copies. This should clear the question in your head about Biblical accuracy.

There are two types of Biblical accuracy. The first type asks if the Bible has been accurately *translated* over the years, however this point instantly becomes irrelevant when discussing the original Hebrew, Aramaic, Greek, and Latin text copies. Once we remove the Biblical translation accuracy issue by eliminating all other Bibles from the discussion, thus leaving only the original Hebrew, Aramaic, Greek, and Latin text copies, then the second issue of Biblical accuracy can be addressed more succinctly.

The Qumran scrolls verify that The Latin Vulgate, The King James and Douay Rheims Bible versions did not substantially change the intent of the words of the Bible other, than for the needs of translating. Some of the issues surrounding the choice of specific words used in these key translations are detailed in the book series *The Science Of God*. But none of this proves that what the Bible says is accurate or true.

The second issue of Biblical accuracy has nothing to do with translations, rather it is only seeking to know if the events in the Bible actually occurred as stated in the Bible. And this second issue of Biblical accuracy is far, far more important than the first.

The importance of you having an extremely clear understanding of the difference between the two types of Biblical accuracy is paramount in your ability to objectively examine the Bible. Without this understanding you will blur the two issues of accuracy and you will likely be able to be manipulated by anyone who has a Biblical agenda, regardless of what that agenda is. However, when you have a clear understanding of this distinction, and that it exists, you can then challenge people who say "the Bible is not accurate" by asking them exactly what they mean when saying that.

Bible Versions Facsimiles

With all of this discussion about the various Bible versions of antiquity, you are probably wondering if any of those exist to this day. The answer is, absolutely yes! There are so many copies of all of what has been discussed so far that it is nearly impossible to track and number it all. Keep in mind that it is not just the Bibles that were printed between AD 1522 and AD 1611, that to this day we still have many original copies of—it goes much further than that! There are also many copies and fragments of copies of many parts of the Bible from many parts of the world with many of them dating back roughly two thousand years or more. This is especially true within the nearly three-thousand-mile radius area surrounding the modern-day Land of Israel.

Today we can add to all of that, that nearly all of these original translations have now been digitally scanned or photographed and are widely distributed electronically. So while there is a limited number of these very abundant texts (tens of thousands of copies of many parts), and translations of them that we consider works of antiquity and which still exist to this day, there is also no shortage of perfect facsimiles of all of that today. Any person who is even mildly dedicated to Bible study can now have their very own Library of perfect digital copies of many of these documents of antiquity, and typically this can be compiled free of charge in a few days' time.

Our modern high-tech world has forever changed Bible study, making it ever easier to research and test, thus leaving all of us without excuse for not knowing. Following are some facsimile examples of the first page of Genesis from some of the Bibles of antiquity that we have been discussing, and are shown together with a text version of their content.

Jerome's Vulgate

1 In principio creavit Deus cælum et terram.

2 Terra autem erat inanis et vacua, et tenebræ erant super faciem abyssi: et spiritus Dei ferebatur super aquas.

3 Dixitque Deus: Fiat lux. Et facta est lux.

4 Et vidit Deus lucem quod esset bona: et divisit lucem a tenebris.

5 Appellavitque lucem Diem, et tenebras Noctem: factumque est vespere et mane, dies unus.

6 Dixit quoque Deus: Fiat firmamentum in medio aquarum: et dividat aquas ab aquis.

7 Et fecit Deus firmamentum, divisitque aquas, quæ erant sub firmamento, ab his, quæ erant super firmamentum. Et factum est ita.

8 Vocavitque Deus firmamentum, Cælum: et factum est vespere et mane, dies secundus.

9 Dixit vero Deus: Congregentur aquæ, quæ sub cælo sunt, in locum unum: et appareat arida. Et factum est ita.

10 Et vocavit Deus aridam Terram, congregationesque aquarum appellavit Maria. Et vidit Deus quod esset bonum.

11 Et ait: Germinet terra herbam virentem, et facientem semen, et lignum pomiferum faciens fructum juxta genus suum, cujus semen in semetipso sit super terram. Et factum est ita.

12 Et protulit terra herbam virentem, et facientem semen juxta genus suum, lignumque faciens fructum, et habens unumquodque sementem secundum speciem suam. Et vidit Deus quod esset bonum.

13 Et factum est vespere et mane, dies tertius.

14 Dixit autem Deus: Fiant luminaria in firmamento cæli, et dividant diem ac noctem, et sint in signa et tempora, et dies et annos:

15 ut luceant in firmamento cæli, et illuminent terram. Et factum est ita.

16 Fecitque Deus duo luminaria magna: luminare majus, ut præesset diei: et luminare minus, ut præesset nocti: et stellas.

17 Et posuit eas in firmamento cæli, ut lucerent super terram,

18 et præessent diei ac nocti, et dividerent lucem ac tenebras. Et vidit Deus quod esset bonum.

19 Et factum est vespere et mane, dies quartus.

20 Dixit etiam Deus: Producant aquæ reptile animæ viventis, et volatile super terram sub firmamento cæli.

21 Creavitque Deus cete grandia, et omnem animam viventem atque motabilem, quam produxerant aquæ in species suas, et omne volatile secundum genus suum. Et vidit Deus quod esset bonum.

22 Benedixitque eis, dicens: Crescite, et multiplicamini, et replete aquas maris: avesque multiplicentur super terram.

23 Et factum est vespere et mane, dies quintus..

German Luther Bible

Das erſte Buch Moſe.

Das 1 Capitel.
Schöpfung der welt.

Am * anfang ſchuf GOtt + himmel und erde.   * Joh. 1, 1. 3.
Col. 1, 16. Ebr. 11, 3. + Pſ. 33, 6.
Pſ. 102, 26.

2. Und die erde war wüſte und leer, und es war finſter auf der tiefe: und * der Geiſt Gottes ſchwebete auf dem waſſer. Pſ. 33, 6.

3. Und GOtt ſprach: * Es werde licht. Und es ward licht.   * 2 Cor. 4, 6.

4. Und GOtt ſahe, daß das licht gut war.   Da * ſchied GOtt das licht von der finſterniß.   * Eſ. 45, 7.

5. Und nante das licht tag, und die finſterniß nacht.   Da ward aus abend und morgen der erſte tag.

6. Und GOtt ſprach: * Es werde eine veſte zwiſchen den waſſern; und die ſey ein unterſchied zwiſchen den waſſern.
* Pſ. 33, 6. Pſ. 136, 5.

7. Da machte GOtt die veſte, und ſchied * das waſſer unter der veſte, von dem waſſer über der veſte. Und es geſchahe alſo.
* Pſ. 104, 3. Pſ. 148, 4. Jer. 10, 12. c. 51, 15.

8. Und GOtt nante die veſte himmel.   Da ward aus abend und morgen der andere tag.

9. Und GOtt ſprach: Es ſamle ſich * das waſſer unter dem himmel an beſondere örter, daß man das trockene ſehe. Und es geſchahe alſo.   * Hiob 38, 8.
Pſ. 33, 7. Pſ. 104, 7. 9. Pſ. 136, 6.

10. Und GOtt nante das trockene erde, und die ſamlung der waſſer nante er meer. Und GOtt ſahe, daß es gut war.

11. Und GOtt ſprach: Es laſſe die erde aufgehen gras und kraut, das ſich beſame; und fruchtbare bäume, da ein jeglicher nach ſeiner art frucht trage, und habe ſeinen eigenen ſamen bey ſich ſelbſt auf erden. Und es geſchahe alſo.

12. Und die erde ließ aufgehen gras und kraut, das ſich beſamete, ein jegliches nach ſeiner art; und bäume, die da frucht trugen, und ihren eigenen ſamen bey ſich ſelbſt hatten, ein jeglicher nach ſeiner art. Und GOtt ſahe, daß es gut war.

13. Da ward aus abend und morgen der dritte tag.

14. Und GOtt ſprach: Es werden * lichter an der veſte des himmels, die da ſcheiden tag und nacht, und geben zeichen, zeiten, tage und jahre. * Pſ. 136, 7. Sir. 43, 2. 9.

15. Und ſeyn lichter an der veſte des himmels, daß ſie ſcheinen auf erden. Und es geſchahe alſo.

16. Und GOtt machte zween große lichter; ein großes licht, das * den tag regiere, und ein kleines licht, das die nacht regiere, dazu auch + ſterne. * 5 M. 4, 19. + Hiob 9, 9.

17. Und GOtt ſetzte ſie an die veſte des himmels, daß ſie ſchienen auf die erde,

18. Und den tag und die nacht regiereten, und * ſchieden licht und finſterniß. Und GOtt ſahe, daß es gut war. * Pſ. 104, 20.

19. Da ward aus abend und morgen der vierte tag.

20. Und GOtt ſprach: Es errege ſich das waſſer mit webynden und lebendigen thieren, und mit * gevögel, das auf erden unter der veſte des himmels fliege. * c. 2, 19.

21. Und GOtt ſchuf große * walfiſche, und allerley thier, das da lebt und webet, und vom waſſer erreget ward, ein jegliches nach ſeiner art; und allerley gefiedertes gevögel, ein jegliches nach ſeiner art. Und GOtt ſahe, daß es gut war.   * Pſ. 104, 26. Hiob 40, 10.

22. Und GOtt ſegnete ſie, und ſprach: * Seyd fruchtbar und mehret euch, und erfüllet das waſſer im meer; und das gevögel mehre ſich auf erden.   * v. 28. c. 8, 17.
c. 9. 1. 7.

A   23. Da

1 Am Anfang schuf Gott Himmel und Erde.

2 Und die Erde war wüst und leer, und es war finster auf der Tiefe; und der Geist Gottes schwebte auf dem Wasser.

3 Und Gott sprach: Es werde Licht! und es ward Licht.

4 Und Gott sah, daß das Licht gut war. Da schied Gott das Licht von der Finsternis

5 und nannte das Licht Tag und die Finsternis Nacht. Da ward aus Abend und Morgen der erste Tag.

6 Und Gott sprach: Es werde eine Feste zwischen den Wassern, und die sei ein Unterschied zwischen den Wassern.

7 Da machte Gott die Feste und schied das Wasser unter der Feste von dem Wasser über der Feste. Und es geschah also.

8 Und Gott nannte die Feste Himmel. Da ward aus Abend und Morgen der andere Tag.

9 Und Gott sprach: Es sammle sich das Wasser unter dem Himmel an besondere Örter, daß man das Trockene sehe. Und es geschah also.

10 Und Gott nannte das Trockene Erde, und die Sammlung der Wasser nannte er Meer. Und Gott sah, daß es gut war.

11 Und Gott sprach: Es lasse die Erde aufgehen Gras und Kraut, das sich besame, und fruchtbare Bäume, da ein jeglicher nach seiner Art Frucht trage und habe seinen eigenen Samen bei sich selbst auf Erden. Und es geschah also.

12 Und die Erde ließ aufgehen Gras und Kraut, das sich besamte, ein jegliches nach seiner Art, und Bäume, die da Frucht trugen und ihren eigenen Samen bei sich selbst hatten, ein jeglicher nach seiner Art. Und Gott sah, daß es gut war.

13 Da ward aus Abend und Morgen der dritte Tag.

14 Und Gott sprach: Es werden Lichter an der Feste des Himmels, die da scheiden Tag und Nacht und geben Zeichen, Zeiten, Tage und Jahre

15 und seien Lichter an der Feste des Himmels, daß sie scheinen auf Erden. Und es geschah also.

16 Und Gott machte zwei große Lichter: ein großes Licht, das den Tag regiere, und ein kleines Licht, das die Nacht regiere, dazu auch Sterne.

17 Und Gott setzte sie an die Feste des Himmels, daß sie schienen auf die Erde

18 und den Tag und die Nacht regierten und schieden Licht und Finsternis. Und Gott sah, daß es gut war.

19 Da ward aus Abend und Morgen der vierte Tag.

20 Und Gott sprach: Es errege sich das Wasser mit webenden und lebendigen Tieren, und Gevögel fliege auf Erden unter der Feste des Himmels.

21 Und Gott schuf große Walfische und allerlei Getier, daß da lebt und webt, davon das Wasser sich erregte, ein jegliches nach seiner Art, und allerlei gefiedertes Gevögel, ein jegliches nach seiner Art. Und Gott sah, daß es gut war.

22 Und Gott segnete sie und sprach: Seid fruchtbar und mehrt euch und erfüllt das Wasser im Meer; und das Gefieder mehre sich auf Erden.

Douay Rheims 1609

THE BOOKE OF
GENESIS, IN HEBREW
BERESITH.

Chap. I.

God createth heauen and earth, and al things therein; distinguishing and beuvtyfing the same; 26. last of al the sixth day he createth man: to vvhom he subiecteth al corporal things of this inferior vvorld.

The first part. Of the creatió of al things.

The Church readeth this booke in her Office from Septuagesima til Passion Sunday.

Also this first chapter & beginning of the second on Easter Eue before Masse.

1 IN the beginning God created heauen, and earth. † And the earth was
2 voide & vacant, and darkenes was vpon the face of the deapth: and the Spirite of God moued ouer the waters. † And God said: Be light made.
3 And light was made. † And God
4 saw the light that it was good: & he
5 diuided the light from the darkenes. † And he called the light, Day, and the darkenes, Night: and there was euening
6 & morning, that made one day. † God also said: Be a firmament made amidst the waters: and let it diuide betwene
7 waters & waters. † And God made a firmament, and diuided the waters, that were vnder the firmament, from those,
8 that were aboue the firmament. And it was so done. † And God called the firmament, Heauen: and there was euening
9 & morning that made the second day. † God also said: Let the waters that are vnder the heauen, be gathered together into one place: and let the drie land appeare. And it was so
10 done. † And God called the drie land, Earth: and the gathering of waters together, he called Seas. And God sawe that
11 it was good. † And said: Let the earth shootforth grene herbes, and such as may seede, & fruite trees yelding fruit after his kinde, such as may haue seede in it selfe vpon the
12 earth. And it was so done. † And the earth brought forth grene

:: The firmament is at the space from the earth to the hieghest starres. the lowest part diuideth betwene the waters on the earth and the waters in the ayer.

S. Aug. li.11.de Gen.ad lit.c.4

:: Likewise heaué is al the space aboue the earth. in whose lowest

14, 15.
17, 24.
Psalm.
32, 6.
135, 5.
Eccli.
10, 1.
Heb.11,
3.

Iob. 38.
Ier. 10,
13.

A   grene

1 In the beginning God created heaven, and earth.

2 And the earth was void and empty, and darkness was upon the face of the deep; and the spirit of God moved over the waters.

3 And God said: Be light made. And light was made.

4 And God saw the light that it was good; and he divided the light from the darkness.

5 And he called the light Day, and the dark-ness Night; and there was evening and morning one day.

6 And God said: Let there be a firmament made amidst the waters: and let it divide the waters from the waters.

7 And god made a firmament, and divided the waters that were under the firmament, from those that were above the firmament, and it was so.

8 And God called the firmament, Heaven; and the evening and morning were the second day.

9 God also said; Let the waters that are under the heaven, be gathered together into one place: and let the dry land appear. And it was so done.

10 And God called the dry land, Earth; and the gathering together of the waters, he called Seas. And God saw that it was good.

11 And he said: let the earth bring forth green herb, and such as may seed, and the fruit tree yielding fruit after its kind, which may have seed in itself upon the earth. And it was so done.

12 And the earth brought forth

King James 1611

The creation   Chap.j.   of the world.

THE
FIRST BOOKE
OF MOSES,
called GENESIS.

CHAP. I.

1 The creation of Heauen and Earth, 3 of the light, 6 of the firmament, 9 of the earth separated from the waters, 11 and made fruitfull, 14 of the Sunne, Moone, and Starres, 20 of fish and fowle, 24 of beasts and cattell, 26 of Man in the Image of God. 29 Also the appointment of food.

I N the beginning God created the heauen, and the Earth.

2 And the earth was without forme, and voyd, and darkenesse was vpon the face of the deepe : and the Spirit of God mooued vpon the face of the waters.

3 And God said, Let there be light : and there was light.

4 And God saw the light, that it was good : and God diuided the light from the darkenesse.

5 And God called the light, Day, and the darkenesse he called Night : and the euening and the morning were the first day.

6 And God said, Let there be a firmament in the midst of the waters : and let it diuide the waters from the waters.

7 And God made the firmament, and diuided the waters, which were vnder the firmament, from the waters, which were aboue the firmament : and it was so.

8 And God called the firmament, heauen : and the euening and the morning were the second day.

9 And God said, Let the waters vnder the heauen be gathered together vnto one place, and let the dry land appeare : and it was so.

10 And God called the dry land, Earth, and the gathering together of the waters called hee, Seas : and God saw that it was good.

11 And God said, Let the Earth bring foorth grasse, the herbe yeelding seed, and the fruit tree, yeelding fruit after his kinde, whose seed is in it selfe, vpon the earth : and it was so.

12 And the earth brought foorth grasse, and herbe yeelding seed after his kinde, and the tree yeelding fruit, whose seed was in it selfe, after his kinde : and God saw that it was good.

13 And the euening and the morning were the third day.

14 And God said, Let there bee lights in the firmament of the heauen, to diuide the day from the night : and let them be for signes and for seasons, and for dayes and yeeres.

15 And let them be for lights in the firmament of the heauen, to giue light vpon the earth : and it was so.

16 And God made two great lights : the greater light to rule the day, and the lesser light to rule the night : he made the starres also.

17 And God set them in the firmament of the heauen, to giue light vpon the earth :

18 And to rule ouer the day, and ouer

1 In the beginning God created the Heauen, and the Earth.

2 And the earth was without forme, and voyd, and darkenesse was vpon the face of the deepe: and the Spirit of God mooued vpon the face of the waters.

3 And God said Let there be light: and there was light.

4 And God saw the light, that it was good: and God diuided the light from the darkenesse.

5 And God called the light, Day, and the darknesse he called Night: and the euening and the morning were the first day. 6 And God said, Let there be a firmament in the midst of the waters: and let it diuide the waters from the waters.

7 And God made the firmament; and diuided the waters, which were vnder the firmament, from the waters, which were aboue the firmament: and it was so.

8 And God called the firmament, Heauen: and the euening and the morning were the second day.

9 And God said, Let the waters vnder the heauen be gathered together vnto one place, and let the dry land appeare: and it was so.

10 And God called the drie land, Earth, and the gathering together of the waters called hee, Seas: and God saw that it was good.

11 And God said, Let the Earth bring foorth grasse, the herbe yeelding seed, and the fruit tree, yeelding fruit after his kinde, whose seed is in it selfe, vpon the earth: and it was so.

12 And the earth brought foorth grasse, and herbe yeelding seed after his kinde, and the tree yeelding fruit, whose seed was in it selfe, after his kinde: and God saw that it was good.

13 And the euening and the morning were the third day.

14 And God said, Let there bee lights in the firmament of the heauen, to diuide the day from the night: and let them be for signes and for seasons, and for dayes and yeeres.

15 And let them be for lights in the firmament of the heauen, to giue light vpon the earth: and it was so.

16 And God made two great lights: the greater light to rule the day, and the lesser light to rule the night: he made the starres also.

17 And God set them in the firmament of the heauen, to giue light vpon the earth: 18 And to rule ouer the day, and ouer the night, and to diuide the light from the darkenesse: and God saw that it was good

While we now have a vast treasure trove of copies to refer to, be cautious with this gift. Pictures of pages are different than textual interpretations of those pictured pages. For the sake of accuracy, our best approach is to obtain actual facsimiles or photo files of the pages of these documents of antiquity, as well as selectable, searchable text copies of them.

"Text copies" as I state it in this chapter has the meaning of the text of the pages being duplicated in a font or typeface similar to the original document, but that are able to be altered with insertable text. There is nothing bad or wrong with such copies, but since they are textual copies it is possible that mistakes could have been made during the conversion to actual editable text. But, they are very good when used *alongside* of the facsimile or pictures of the pages of those versions because they are crisp clear text and they are *text-searchable*.

Chapter and Verse

When you begin comparing Bibles side by side, you might notice some discrepancies between chapter and verse from one Bible to another. This is another one of those little things that makes people doubt the accuracy of the various translation versions, but don't let this distract you. While the chapters and verses might have some differences between them, the text is still the same. The chapter and verse indicators were added long after the original Hebrew, Aramaic, Greek, and Latin text copies were written. When these accounts were first written they were simply telling what happened and they likely never imagined that their writings would become part of a controversial book that would place their texts into chapter and verse notations for the entire world to read.

The idea of Bible *chapters* was not imagined until the thirteenth century and wasn't really applied until the fourteenth century. And verse numbers where not added until the fifteenth century. The reason that both of these divisions were added was for referencing purposes.

We are so accustomed to citing chapter and verse today that it is hard for us to imagine the text without it. The Bible has *four* organizational divisions. The first is the *Testaments*, the second is the *book names* in the Bible, the third is *chapter divisions*, and the fourth is *verse divisions* within the chapters. Each of these divisions is a gift given by those who created them and implemented them. It would be very difficult to discuss the Bible with any efficiency without these divisions. These Biblical organizational divisions coupled with the 1440s Gutenberg printing revolution are rivaled only by our modern digital technology.

The *Testaments*, *book names*, *chapters*, and *verses* have also aided in assuring translation and version accuracy. Once these methods of notation were fully implemented, people who were *not* fulltime Bible scholars could easily locate and review any text that was a topic of conversation. These particular division methods are preferred over page numbers because they allow for varying formatting of the text in any language to all be synchronized during research, thus rendering page numbers meaningless. This makes it possible for us today to dig into the text as if we are all scholars and see for ourselves if the modern Bible versions match the versions of antiquity and the original Hebrew, Aramaic, Greek, and Latin text copies. These divisions were the final check system that put the Bible into the hands of the entire world for intense scrutiny. That is of course until everything was digitized and made available electronically.

No document on the face of this Earth has ever been challenged with the same meticulous level of scrutiny and met the challenge undaunted as does the Bible. The translations are accurate, especially when used collectively. As for inerrancy of the text, from a translation standpoint, absolutely not. There are too many nuances in words and language to claim *translation* inerrancy. But regarding the *content* being inerrant, that is quite a different subject and task to take on.

Chapter 11

The Information Contained In the Bible

Most of what has been discussed in this book up to this point was not about the *content* of the Bible, other than the part where it was pointed out that Salvation is for all of mankind, therefore, the **Bible** is for **all** of mankind, even though the Bible follows only "God's People". The naming and origins and assembly of the Bible discussed up to this point have little to do with the Bible's content. Once we understand the basic assembly of the Bible and the high accuracy of most translations and the fact that we can still go back to original source texts and also other texts of antiquity, we can then begin to consider as to whether or not the content of the text is accurate. When looking into the accuracy of the Bible's *content* we must first ask, why does the Bible follow this particular group of people?

God's People

In order for us to properly mentally receive and analyze the information in the Bible, we have to understand the ultimate point to the assembly of the overall information contained in it. The history listed in the Bible follows a particular group of people for two specific reasons: The first reason is that they are the ones who actually recorded their history and carried that history through their good times and through their bad times, and they added to it as new critical events occurred. They are also the ones who are said to have assembled the Bible in the form of the Septuagint—an event that is documented *outside* of the Bible.

The other reason that the Bible follows this particular group of people is that it was through the blood-line of "God's people" from which the Savior was to come, and according to the New Testament *did* in fact come. With this understanding, we can free our minds of needing to ask why is there such a lack of information in the Bible about the many other peoples of the world, but here we must also not forget about the Bible's long and detailed list of the origins of the nations. If Salvation had come through a different bloodline, then the so-called "God's people" would not be in the Bible, and the Bible would have the history of a different people through whom Salvation would have been brought forth. In other words, the only reason "God's People", who happen to be the Israelites, are spoken of in the Bible is because they are who God chose to use for a bloodline due to the strong dedication to God from only a few of those people.

The Bible is not the history of some random people that ultimately led to the arrival of the Savior, it is a specific account of a people who were once chosen because of the dedication of their forefathers.

"God's people" began with a promise to Abraham from God that Abraham's bloodline would become "many nations". And it is Abraham's bloodline that the Savior, who was promised to Adam and Eve, was to come through. The promise went through Abraham's son Isaac, and then through Isaac's son Jacob. And it is through the sons of Jacob that the term "God's people" came about. But even before Abraham, we have to consider Noah of the Ark. Noah had three sons and one of them was named Shem. It is through Shem that the Salvation bloodline went through because Shem was faithful, and he passed his faithful learning on down to his descendent-offspring-grandson, Abraham (or Abram at that time).

When a famine struck the land where Jacob and his sons and daughter lived, they eventually went to Egypt to live because of the famine. The Bible explains that Jacob was at some point renamed "Israel" by "The Lord", and thus the sons of Jacob and their descendants from that point forward were referred to as "Israel" or "Israelites".

The Israelites descended through Shem, Noah's son (or Sem, as in "Semites". You might be more familiar with the term anti-Semitic.) The key names in succession are Noah to Shem, then Terah to Abraham to Isaac to Jacob/Israel.

The Israelites flourished in Egypt, and when the reigning Pharaoh who invited them in had died, that Pharaoh's successor did not share the same affinity towards the Israelites as his father had. In fear of the rapidly increasing numbers of Israelites and the sheer force of what they were becoming, the new Pharaoh commanded that the Israelites must be enslaved. Then as the story goes, after many years of being captive slaves in Egypt, God promised that he would redeem them with an outstretched arm and with mighty acts of judgment and told them, as found in Leviticus chapter 26, "I will take you as my own people, and I will be your God". This is the point when the Israelites became "God's people".

This occurred when the Israelites were eventually freed from Egypt through a series of events or plagues that finally forced the

Egyptian Pharaoh of that time to release them. From that point on, the Israelites also became known as "God's people."

What is a "Story"?

The Bible is full of "stories." A common underlying sentiment of the word "story" is that it is an invented tale that, while it may mimic real life, is entirely fictitious. When we read "Bible stories" to children and then later fail to teach them the full details of those historical accounts, we then feed the belief that those "stories" are only fiction. But many people, when they are adults, generally do not consider that there is more than one kind of "story" when it comes to the Bible.

There are a few different mental separations to consider regarding "Stories" in the Bible. Since most Bibles are reasonably accurately translated and many events in the Bible can be proven to have occurred through written documents and tangible evidence outside of the Bible, it clears a great deal of fog surrounding the Bible and its stories.

Some things listed in the Bible have ample evidence of being actual accounts, but other things have little or no specific evidence. Ruins of some of the places mentioned in the Bible have been found, and evidence of some of the described activity occurring in those cities has also been found. But how do we know that the Bible was not just a bunch of stories made up about these ruins and had been written *after* the fact?

We can claim that these stories were invented and written after the events occurred, but that is unlikely since there is more than a couple of Bible stories where there are written accounts as well as tangible evidence of being real events. There are just too many pieces of physical evidence, and there are just too many copies of the Biblical text from too many of the original Hebrew, Aramaic, Greek, and Latin text copies for all of the stories to be fictitious. If all stories in the Bible were fictitious, it is unlikely that there would be more than a couple of copies of any of the accounts. Since there are more than a few copies from various regions that detail some of the events, it is highly *unlikely* that those events did not occur. It is just not logical to discount those events and imply that somehow they are *all* fictitious. Yet, even when we finally accept that the provable documentable events as described in the various Bible stories had actually occurred and are true, we still have other "story" types to consider.

Bible Story Types

1. Spiritual aspects

2. Miracles

3. Prophecies

4. Proverbs and Psalms

5. Parables

6. Provable documentable events

There is little point in discussing the *Provable documentable events* in this context because they are provable and documented. We can also immediately remove the *Parables* that Christ told and *Proverbs* and *Psalms* from the discussion, because those are generally *not* intended to be actual true stories of specific events and are thus obvious in their purpose of being fabricated, though many do speak of real events. *Proverbs* and *Psalms* writings are similar to Jesus' *Parables* in that the statements made within them are examples and analogies and are generally intended to be lessons for the readers. This leaves us with the three remaining story types, *Spiritual*, *Miracles*, and *Prophecies* that we need to focus our attention on regarding questioning Biblical "stories".

Three Points of Accuracy

We discussed the inerrancy of Bible translations and we found that while the translations might not be able to technically be referred to as "inerrant", they are in fact very accurate to the original Hebrew, Aramaic, Greek, and Latin text copies, which is the first point of accuracy.

The second point of accuracy is whether or not the events stated in the Bible actually occurred as stated, or at least close enough to the description of events stated so as to be considered credible accounts.

And the final and third point of accuracy questions if certain things are true or possible, such as the idea of Salvation or even if God actually exists.

But our problem is that we generally do not realize that these mental divisions exist regarding the points of accuracy or even that they need to be considered when analyzing the text of the Bible. We are often too insistent on each of us being *right*, rather than us all collectively working to find the correct *true* answers to our questions. We typically want it *our own* way rather than the *true* way. But again, these Biblical debates do force us to answer the tough questions about our perspectives regarding our questions about Biblical matters.

When someone says that we should believe in God to avoid Hell, it is very revealing regarding their life philosophy. In fact, even if they are atheists and claim that people only believe in God because of their fear of Hell, it exposes a great deal about the atheist person's life philosophy. This is true in either case because *we* want to see things the way *we* want to see things, rather than wanting to honor God simply because the Creator Created all things. We often take the position that we'll go to Hell because we know we have been behaving badly, so instead we try to honor God, accept Christ, and believe we receive Salvation. But there are also those of us who outright reject God because God and the consequences of God do not agree with our life philosophy. In other words, we think, "I will not honor anyone who has power over me and can potentially punish me" and therefore we choose to not believe at all, or so we say.

Too many of both believers and non-believers alike attribute the stories told in the Bible to fiction, but of course not all people do so. Rational people realize that most historical accounts detailed in the Bible likely occurred as stated, but they might not accept the third point of accuracy, which includes things like Salvation being real or that God actually exists.

When you consider the three points of accuracy you will notice that different people will believe each point differently. Some will believe that the accounts occurred, but could not possibly be accurately relayed through over two-thousand years of translations, and some of them will outright reject the God/Salvation aspects. There are also many Christians who believe the God/Salvation aspect, but they reject the accuracy of the translation and reject the possibility that the accounts are all real true historical events.

The three points of accuracy that I refer to are *Translational, Historical,* and *Spiritual.* Rejecting all three points of accuracy is irrational and deliberately ignorant. But even rejecting either of *Translational* or *Historical* is also irrational. The *Translational* accuracy speaks for itself as discussed throughout the previous ten chapters. These following chapters are more about the *Historical* accuracy, which has ample evidence of antiquity— evidence that is increasing daily.

Of the three accuracy points, the only one that comes close to not being logically irrational when we reject it is the *Spiritual.* Some people might be offended by any suggestion that rejecting the *Spiritual* point is not irrational, but this book is not intended to force anyone's beliefs. In these later chapters of this book, we are dealing mostly with the accuracy of tangible evidence and understanding that evidence. Those Biblical issues that are spiritual in nature are a bit different and are briefly discussed as well.

Logic of Evidence

Imagine for a moment if movie film had been invented during the time of Christ, and the Crucifixion had actually been filmed with audio and could be watched today. What specifically would that prove to us? Would it prove Salvation exists? Would it prove that it was the prophesied Savior that was Crucified?

Many Christians would probably automatically respond with a resounding, "Yes, that would be proof of Salvation and of Jesus". But upon further thought they would have to retract that answer and realize that even a news movie of the actual Christ being Crucified and dying is proof of little other than that a man was nailed to a cross and he died, and even the death part could not be verified with such video. As truly amazing as that would be to have such a movie, it is little better than a written eyewitness account, or for that matter, it is little better than a living eyewitness's verbal account.

While issues surrounding your own Salvation are your own decision, here in our using the death of Christ as an example and asking if it proves Salvation, we are not wondering if Salvation is real. Rather we are wondering if our imagined movie of the death of Christ on a cross *proves* in any way that the man in our imaginary movie is the one who was prophesied to be Salvation for the people, and if he actually died. *This pertains to **only the history** of Salvation and the Savior, but **not** as to whether or not Salvation is real, so the reality of Salvation is another mental division for you to understand and keep in mind.

What we are trying to establish here is: Does our example news-movie prove that the promised Savior mentioned throughout the Bible is actually the man in our imagined movie of the Crucifixion? The answer to this is **no**, it would not *prove* that the man in our movie was the Savior even if he actually was. Therefore, written accounts are equal to an actual movie with sound. Now this could be viewed a bit differently if the people seen in the movie were walking around alive together with us today and could give us personal verbal eyewitness testimony. But since they are not here to give us live eyewitness testimony, the movie would be all that we have available. Further, some people living back then who took part in the crucifixion did not even believe that Jesus was our Salvation. If they had, then they likely would not have crucified Him.

But even if the people in the movie were alive and here with us today, a movie with audio mentioning the name of Jesus would still not prove that the man on the Cross in the news-movie was in fact *the* "Jesus". They could have taken any man and nailed him to the cross and called him Jesus. A movie is no better than the words that they wrote roughly two thousand years ago. And even if they were alive today and gave eyewitness testimony, it still does not prove the He was the Savior, it still only proves that a man was crucified.

"Proof" is a cumulative effort that requires the use of human logic. Once an event occurs and is in the past, there is no definitive proof of any event because our human rationale can and will deny that evidence *when we have chosen* to not believe it. It simply does not matter how strong the evidence is, unless we are all witnessing something, live, first-hand together. Everything thereafter is of limited value and is only evidence.

It is our human ability to logic our way through evidence and compile it into logical groupings and then attempt to rebuild the events that may have occurred using the evidence as a form of verification of the events. We then must weigh that evidence and cumulatively and personally decide if we feel that the events, in fact, actually occurred. This is exactly what occurs in courtrooms and in jury deliberations around the world.

There is much documentation of people being persecuted, after the Crucifixion of Christ, for having taken part in Christian meetings because they had Christian beliefs. Now, this in itself does not prove the Bible to be true, but it does confirm that as far as about two thousand years ago people were persecuted for following what is written in the Gospels and in the epistles of the Bible. If you choose to deny that this is true then you might as well deny that Abraham Lincoln was a president of the United States, and you might as well deny that your great-great-grandparents ever lived. And after your parents have passed, you might as well deny that your parents ever lived. At some point, we must accept written history as acceptable testimony when it is verifiable by means of cross-referential historical documents and when it agrees with other facts, otherwise *no* history whatsoever has any validity to us at all, and it never can if we reject written accounts.

We simply cannot be taken credibly if we reject the historical accounts listed in the Bible. For instance, to deny that this "Jesus" person was crucified is outright foolish. You can debate the deification of Jesus The Christ and the claim that he is the "only begotten son of God" and that he was the result of a virgin birth. But to deny that he existed and was crucified is a foolish position based upon much historical documentation *outside* of the Bible.

There are detailed debates that argue whether Jesus was nailed to a cross, versus being nailed to a tree, and those types of things can legitimately be debated because the text in some Bible versions is not explicit in that regard. And depending upon our interpretation of any version that we are interpreting, it might allow for such variances. But to debate that the general events did not occur will make a fool of us when we embark on that path of debate with nearly any serious scholar who is a detailed historian of the history from that general region of the globe during that era of time.

Written statements carry a great deal of weight in our court systems, and when corroborated with other written witness testimony, we can typically determine with a great amount of certainty that some particular activity actually occurred when we put aside our biases. Now consider that this legalistic Crucifixion case has been in the court of public scrutiny for about two-thousand years and has yet to be adequately defeated.

The *inability* to adequately defeat a strong case is very important in understanding if an event actually occurred.

A case can appear solid with no chance of being exposed as fraudulent, but if a single *credible* piece of evidence is brought forth, it can make the entire case crumble to its defeat. To date, there have been no credible rebuttals of the Crucifixion of Jesus. So, after a couple of thousand years, it is time for everyone to realize that the Crucifixion actually occurred. The entire Bible does not share the same level of certainty, but much of it does come close.

The same level of logic of evidence doesn't apply to *Proverbs and Psalms* and such, or to *Parables* for the obvious reason that those are generally a prayer or song or are intended as fictitious teaching examples. But the logic of evidence does apply to *Provable documentable events* and to *Miracles* and *Prophecies*.

Miracles

What is a miracle? When speaking of miracles in the Bible, we often think of those that Jesus did that are mentioned in the Gospels of the New Testament, but there are also *miracles* in the Old Testament. In a non-Biblical sense, we use the term "miracle" when we are astonished by something, such as a person who has had the lifelong habit of living in a risky or wild manner, but they then suddenly and permanently change their behavior and we say "it's a "miracle!" However, if behavioral changes are to be considered *Miracles*, it would partly fall into the *Spiritual* category of events. While these sorts of personal changes in people did occur in the Bible, they are not specifically the types of *miraculous* events that pique our interest regarding the book you are now reading.

We typically think of Biblical miracles as extremely unusual events, usually with some level of divine intervention. The term miracle comes from a Latin word *miraculum*. The *mira* part of the word means *amazing* or *surprising*. And the *culum* part of the word means to *admire*. The word, *miraculum* or miracle, basically means to see something very unusually astonishing and realize that there is something special or very unique about the event. When we speak of Biblical miracles, most people will immediately think of the miracles performed by Jesus. But miracles include events like parting the Red Sea, or making water come out of a rock or having a pillar, of fire hold back Pharaoh and his army.

Some of the miracles in the Bible were rather harsh and did not turn out favorable to those on the wrong side of those harsh miracles. Miracles are one of those aspects where it is good to understand that there are mental divisions. In the case of miracles, we often do not consider the plagues in Egypt as "miracles". We have mentally divided the plagues off as something negative, but not as miracles, yet they actually are miracles. Miracles that have negative ramifications for some people are still miracles nonetheless, and they share the same miraculous validity as the miracles that had only good results.

There are then two types of miracles, *Evidentiary* and *Spiritual*. Our example of a person living wildly and then suddenly changing can be proven by the evidence of change that we see in the person, and in that case it is an *evidentiary* change and it is important for them as an individual. But it is a *behavioral* change that is attributed to *Spirit* or self, rather than an actual *Evidentiary* miracle.

The other miracle type is *Evidentiary*. *Evidentiary* miracles don't involve people's feelings and are physical in nature, meaning that they typically left evidence but were not dependent upon people's feelings or their soul or spirit. Parting the Red Sea is an example of *Evidentiary* miracles as are the plagues of Egypt and the rising of the dead, etc.

Many of the *Evidentiary* miracles have some level of physical evidence remaining, and that evidence is corroborated by written eyewitness testimony of the time. This puts these events on the same level as the *Provable documentable events*. But the *Evidentiary Miracles* differ in that they are very unusual events that are, to us humans, extraordinary to the point of our disbelief. But when weighing *Evidentiary Miracles* on the same scale and by the same standards as *Provable documentable events*, they rise to the same standards and only differ due to their unique nature together with our typical unwillingness to accept that they could have actually occurred.

Some of the *Evidentiary Miracles* had an additional point of corroboration in that they were foretold of in various *Prophecies*. After some time had elapsed and the prophecies had been fulfilled and left physical evidence, those original events were then further corroborated by written eyewitness accounts.

Prophecy Stories

Can prophecies be proven through logic of evidence? And what exactly are "prophecies" anyway? Prophecies are often misunderstood in our modern culture. "Prophets" are thought to be people who have some unique ability to tell the future like a fortune teller claims to, but this is not true.

If we are to believe the actual historical events listed in the Bible, then we must take serious consideration of the *Prophecies* and of the *Prophets*. The prophets were not randomly inventing their prophecies, nor did they have some unique ability to see the future. The prophets typically either had a visitation or were taken away and shown things or had visions.

It is mostly impossible to prove a prophecy that has not yet been fulfilled. Proving one after it has already occurred is often attributed to "chance". In other words, when someone makes a prediction of some peculiar event and that event actually occurs, we then typically attribute it to "a lucky guess".

There have been many non-Biblical prophecies made over the years by many people, and if those prophecies were vague enough or general enough in nature, then at some point in the future, an event is likely to occur that will fit the prophecy well enough to claim that the prophecy has been fulfilled. When someone makes enough *broad* statements of what they imagine might occur in the future, then many of those prophecies are bound to be thought of as "fulfilled" when given enough time for reasonably similar events to occur in the eyes of gullible people.

But if prophecies are specific and detailed and sometimes even dated, then it increases their credibility exponentially, thus removing them from fortune-teller status and placing those prophecies squarely in the official "prophecy" category. But even this could be attributed to luck because random coincidences do occur from time to time. However, if *specific* and *detailed* prophecies are fulfilled and this occurs more than a couple of times with many different prophecies, then the **odds** *of it being luck* in guessing at the future decrease to a point where "luck" can no longer be legitimately claimed by any reasonable statistician-mathematician, or any other person for that matter.

When enough *accurate* prophecies are fulfilled *accurately*, we come to a point where denial is absurd. However, we still might not know for sure whether or not the so-called prophecy was actually written *before* the alleged fulfillment of that prophecy. This puts us in a position of having to find logical ways to determine if the prophecy was, in fact, proclaimed *before* the events occurred that are responsible for the fulfillment of the prophecy. Here is the pivotal point about prophecies: If we cannot determine that the account was written *before* the fulfillment of the prophecy, it makes the claimed prophetic statements lack credibility.

Here is another mental separation point for you to keep in mind. If a prophecy was supposedly made but cannot be verifiably placed *before* the fulfillment of that prophecy, it does **not** make the claimed *fulfillment* event that occurred to be considered untrue. Even if someone was trying to pretend to be a prophet and wrote the "prophecy" *after* the fulfillment event occurred, the event itself still can often be proven to have occurred if it in fact actually occurred, especially if it left physical evidence. Being able to mentally separate the legitimacy of a prophecy, versus the legitimacy of an event, is very important to remember and practice discerning.

Testing to see if *Provable documentable events* were actually prophesied **beforehand** takes a bit of textual logic to determine. The Jesus prophecies are fairly easy to prove that they were written beforehand because there are so many of them. The assembly of the Septuagint in the third century BC (that's roughly 200-300 years *before* Jesus' birth) is documented by *outside* history. The Septuagint was used by people of the day, likely including Jesus himself. This means that **after the prophecies were written down**, we have evidence of them being acknowledged before The Christ was born, due to the timing of the Septuagint translation and the outside references to it. Any historical references about the Septuagint that were made **before** Christ was born testify to the prophecies about Jesus and that they clearly were stated *before* Jesus was born. This is critically important to understand regarding Old Testament prophecies that pertain to the New Testament, which were actually provably prophesied during the Old Testament era and provably recorded in the Old Testament.

Since the Septuagint is the Hebrew Old Testament, we have reasonably strong evidence of the timeline arrangement of the documenting of the prophecies themselves and of the specific events that had been prophesied that actually subsequently occurred in the New Testament. Since the Septuagint was assembled *between* the Old Testament events and the start of the New Testament events, we know through historical documentation that that assembly took place *before* the birth of Jesus. This means that we have proof that the Savior prophecies were written **before** Jesus The Christ was actually born.

What we need to each ourselves consider is, do we believe that the prophecies have been fulfilled through the witness' accounts listed in the four Gospels? The evidence that occurred matches the actual prophecies quite well. But still, each of us must decide on our own, what our personal conclusions are regarding the Old Testament prophecies telling of the coming Savior, Jesus The Christ. Regardless of what we each choose to believe, it will not and cannot change what actually occurred. So, we can personally decide that it's all a stretch of our own imagination and that it is hard to believe, but that particular path of thinking has no bearing whatsoever as to whether or not the prophecies and the fulfillment events actually occurred.

There are many seemingly minor prophecies in the Bible that were fulfilled during the timespan of Old Testament, but there are also many that were fulfilled upon Christ's arrival, lifetime, death, and subsequent rising from the dead and ascension as detailed in the New Testament. There are also many prophecies yet to be fulfilled, such as some of those in the book of Revelation.

When we consider the amount of written testimony and then we use sound logic to examine the timelines regarding prophecies and the fulfillment of those prophecies, the evidence is really quite compelling in its indication that the events all occurred as stated and can easily be regarded as historical fact. However, this still does not address the purely *Spiritual* aspects, which is perhaps the most important part of it all if the Bible is to be believed.

We all must consider that many thousands, and perhaps millions, of people have scrutinized the prophecies leading to the New Testament events and have not been able to discount them adequately. In fact, most people who have sought to research these questions arrive at the same conclusions and have been doing so for about two-thousand years. This in itself is proof of nothing other than that the proofs that lead to the conclusion that—many of the Old Testament prophecies were actually fulfilled in the New Testament. Some aspects of these thoroughly-inspected prophecies and fulfillments touch on the *Spiritual* type story.

Spiritual Stories

Spiritual type stories are often difficult for us to prove because they leave no scientific tangible evidence of having occurred. The Spiritual/God aspects of history have to do with souls being saved from having to spend eternity in Hell and absent of God. Sins are not tangible, but the results of the actions of those sins typically are, which brings us to topics surrounding "morality".

We get trapped in our modern definitions of the words that we use in our language. And matters of spirit, since they are not tangible, leave many of us at a loss. So, let's examine a few of these words.

Spirit can be translated as *gentle, wind,* or *breeze,* or more appropriately *breath.* Words and their development are one of those chicken-versus-egg areas where we need to logic through and determine what came first, the *word,* or the *concept* of the word. Since *spirit* is not a scientifically tangible aspect, it is compared to what we think of as *wind* or *breath* in that it is invisible and cannot be touched in the way a rock can be touched. Which when you think about it, *breath* or *breeze* is a very good comparison to the concept of a *soul* if you are trying to convey the concept of a soul to another person who is not familiar with the idea of a "soul" or spirit.

When we allow ourselves to dig deep enough within our own thinking, we find that our biases are often due to our fears. Those who are afraid or have fear of death in them are more likely to discount much of the Bible as being *not* credible. We often build our discounting of the Bible upon our own personal view of the *Spiritual* type stories. Much of what we personally conclude about the Bible has to do with the order in which we see it, or how we understand it.

Some of us have behaved badly for a long time and we seek to mentally prove to ourselves that the entire Bible is nothing more than fictitious stories, thus we delegitimize the concept of Hell within our own mind to avoid thinking about potential ramifications for our behavior. But, of course, such denial has no bearing on what is or is not true regarding Hell.

For many people who have not behaved badly and are generally very respectful people, it is not so much our fears that cause us to question the viability of the *Spiritual* type stories, rather it is the technique with which we view the overall information. *Spiritual* type stories in the Bible are intertwined with the *Provable documentable events*, and if we are unable to validate the spiritual aspects in our own mind, then it typically affects our personal conclusions regarding the *Provable documentable events*.

Part of this issue is due to the way we have been taught. If you have read some of my other books you have likely noticed the discussions regarding *blind*-faith versus *true*-faith. Blind-faith is not wrong, but it can be dangerous if people follow the wrong shepherd. The "shepherd" reference is regarding the "Good Shepherd", or Jesus The Christ, mentioned in the New Testament. If you follow the proper instructions of the "Good Shepherd", that's Jesus, then you will go down the right path even if you have only blind-faith. However, if you should come upon a not-so-good-shepherd and follow that shepherd with your blind-faith, then you can easily be led astray. This of course goes beyond Biblical matters and is true of *all* things in life, such as what we see with children whose parents are often absent and who allow them to hang out on the streets unsupervised at all times.

When we are told that "You should just believe in God. And this is what the Bible says..." and we follow this advice, we then have "blind faith". This blind-faith way of seeing the Bible causes us to look *first* at the *Spiritual* type stories before we do any review of the *Provable documentable events*. I am not suggesting that this is specifically wrong, but rather I am illustrating that it can be dangerous and possibly misleading when the wrong shepherds are leading you *and* you have not studied and understood *all* of the information.

When children are being taught Bible "stories" and the information is not properly elaborated on as they age, these children then will grow up *not* understanding the real-life details of the Bible's text. The Salvation message is driven into us at a very young age, and through preachers, teachers, and parents the Salvation message is reinforced, and we are often told that the Salvation message is the only *important* part. Since we have then been offered the *ultimate* answer to the problem, there is an underlying feeling within us that there is no additional need to read the Bible, and thus all incentive is lost. Then as a result, as young adults, we lack adequate ability to be able to articulate the details of the Bible when we are challenged on our thoughts, regardless of which belief we happened to adopt regarding whether or not the Bible is true. This is not about us being able to make our case to other people, rather it is us being able to adequately make our case *within our own head* regardless of our chosen belief.

Eventually our blind-faith view will cause us to be challenged on issues of morality and what *morality* actually is and means. Since our blind-faith perspective has not prepared us to articulate our position adequately when the question of morality arises regarding the Bible, our blind-faith fails us, thus making us unable to defend our position on "morality" and *why* it exists.

What Is Morality?

The word "morality" comes from the word *moral*, and the origin of *moral* means *custom* or *customary* in its native language. This means that to be "moral" is nothing more than following the customs of the people in whose community you are living or are staying. By this standard, or "morality", we then can rob, kill, and plunder and be considered "moral" if we are in one of those areas where good behavior is absent. But what is "good behavior"?

Behavioral matters clearly fall under the *Spiritual* type story category of the story types listed in this chapter. The effects from *behavioral* issues and activities generally result in *Provable documentable events.* When we enter life with a blind-faith approach, we tend to view the entire Bible in only a *moral behavior* manner when the Bible is actually far more than that.

When we see all of the bad behavior listed in the Bible, it causes us to group the overall information together in our mind and we associate the documented bad behavior together with the entire Bible overall, making the Bible appear as somewhat irrational because we have been taught that "the Bible is good" in a rose-colored-view sort of way. These two perspectives do not reconcile in our heads, and thus we cast the Bible as fictitious because "How could a loving God allow that to happen?" in the Bible.

People have debates in public forums about whether God is needed in order for "morality" to exist. The argument being that God is not needed in order for morality to exist and that humans will generally automatically eventually evolve to behave in a "moral" manner because society holds immoral behavior accountable. But this then leaves us with a troubling area regarding defining the limits of "morality".

In the beginning of the previous section the chicken-versus-egg topic was brought up in regard to what comes first, the word or the concept behind the word? Our general societal definition of "moral" does not match the word's origin meaning. Morality is discussed as if there are hard parameters that guide its limits, but those parameters are the practices that are acceptable to society, and this does in fact match the origin meaning of the word. Yet, we tend to think of it in our minds as more definitive than what is "socially acceptable". When a society works to make something such as abortion or "lifestyle choices" morally acceptable, then is that recently accepted behavior acceptable regarding what we would *previously* have thought of as "moral"? By origin definition, to be "moral" is to comply with the customary behavior of the people of the area, and thus such lifestyle choices then become "morally" acceptable when using *that* standard.

But underneath this "moral" definition lies our very obvious awareness that these behaviors are somehow different than most issues of "morality" and must then be **_forced_** onto society and into the definition of "moral" in order for it to be accepted by the general populous. This then leads us to wonder, is morality *constant* or is it okay for morality to change or to evolve?

If morality evolves into the practice of killing your neighbor as being "morally acceptable", then is that killing to be considered "moral"? Does the evolution of societal morality ever stop? Does morality have any hard parameters than are not to be breached—ever?

When we think of morality and defying morality, that is when the topic of *sin* enters the conversation. But what is "sin"? The general understanding of sin is that when we defy morality or defy God we are then in "sin", or have sinned or are sinners. So let's look a bit more at the word "sin". *Sin* means *without* or *empty* or *void* or *absence*. But if we sin, and if sin does actually mean "*empty*" or "*absence*" or any other indicator of lack or shortage in any way, then what is it that we are indicting that we are lacking when discussing "sin"?

This is where "God" enters the picture and this goes all the way back to Genesis when Adam and Eve were removed from the Garden. As the story goes, Adam and Eve were no longer able to be in God's presence in the same way that they previously had been, and thus they are *without* God. They had sinned and that lack of God was passed down through their offspring for all generations. But then God promised them a Savior that would come to their aid and restore their former position and thus take away their *sin*, *lack*, or *absence*. This would allow them to once again be with God as they had formerly been when the prophesied and appointed time for the Savior was to come.

So, is morality *constant* and did God say, thou shalt be *moral?* How did the word "moral" come to be the particular word used for the concept of what we see as "morality"? This chicken-versus-egg issue asks, how specifically is the word "moral" connected to *good behavior* and the Bible?

"Moral" basically means customary behavior, so we must look at from which society the term arose. The Latin term "*moralis*" is *custom,* and *custom* is from Latin *consuescere* which indicates self-destruction. What we are attempting to drill down to is, why is the word "moral" the particular word used to describe behavioral standards? Based upon the various above words' etymologies, it's easy to see that the term "moral" is ultimately indicating that you will cause an end to yourself if you fail to abide by the customary standards of something or someone—that is to say the "morals" of something or someone. What we need to establish is, what behavior will put an end to us? And why is that behavior so dangerous? And what, or who, is the something or someone?

I have heard people make claims such as, "God is against adultery but is for genocide", but such points are wrongly made and are done so without consideration of the **why** factor within the debate. When assuming that God would do this, we have to assume that there is a "God" as we discuss the particular topic. This is one of those mental separation issues we often fail to realize. When presenting the comparison of being against adultery but for genocide, you don't get to make up your own rules in the debate. If we're going to claim that God does not exist because we cannot believe that someone would be against adultery but yet be for genocide, we then should not be allowed to even discuss the topic because we just indicated that God does not exist and therefore we cannot make the claim that God is against adultery but is for genocide, because in that case, there is no God to be *for* or *against* either.

If such a comparison is made, then the only rational way that we can discuss the apparent anomaly would be for the person making the claim, to only make such a comparison under the assumption that God *does* exist, and at no point in the conversation can the idea of a non-existent God be brought into the discussion whatsoever. Dismissing God creates an irrational conversation in this case. The point here is that when such a comparison is made *accusing* "God" of irrational behavior, then "God" *must* be included in all attempts to rationalize or de-rationalize the comparison. This leaves us with two choices or positions: The first position is that *God is utterly irrational* and just arbitrarily decides as to what is good and what is bad regarding humans. This would mean that there is no logic in any Godly action and thus we as humans cannot figure it out because it is random and therefore we must just shut up and abide by such arbitrary "rules".

The second position in the debate is that *God is completely rational* and there are *specific reasons* for all of God's actions and God's "moral" guidelines. Here again, we must define the mental separation between *God's guidelines* and *God's actions*.

To blindly liken God's guidelines with God's actions is very dishonest. Failing to separate God's guidelines from God's actions is like saying that "God is against adultery, but God is for genocide." This is essentially implying that God said "Thou *shalt not* commit adultery, but thou *must* commit genocide."

The reason that someone would dare to suggest that God is for genocide is because God instructed his people to wipe out the inhabitants of an entire city. But what is missing in this particular debate of–*God being against adultery but being for genocide*–is **context**. That sentiment fails to ask, **why** would God ask his people to carry out such a horrific task? And it is the failure to ask that **why**-question that invites irrational statements to be made such as "God is against adultery, but is for genocide." Ask yourself, why would a "good" God ask his people to wipe out inhabitants of an entire city? In the modern era you can think along the lines of when the police are arresting someone and it is caught on camera and the video is passed around causing outrage, but only the arrest part is caught on camera and not the offence that the perpetrator is being arrested for, which will paint a very different picture.

This brings us back to "morality". Morality is ultimately a set of rules by which we are to abide. So "morality", as we think of it today, is not really an evolving set of social standards. It is actually a set of *specific* standards that command respect and care of others, and which also rejects harming others *unless* they violate the respect and care of others. Thus, if some people are randomly murdering people without just cause, then is it right that those who are doing the murdering should be allowed to continue? Or is it acceptable to stop them, via killing them if needed? Your answer here should answer the question as to why God would have had the people wipe out the inhabitants of an entire city.

Let's see whether or not this so-called "God" is irrational or unjust and arbitrarily murders and commits genocide on an entire city without cause. Consider the story of Sodom and Gomorrah. The inhabitants of these two cities are recorded to have been so cruel and evil that they were to be destroyed at the hand of God. Then as the story goes, Abraham was told of this impending destruction and took God to task on the subject. Here is the text from the Douay Rheims Bible, Genesis, chapter 18:

"20 And the Lord said: The cry of Sodom and Gomorrah is multiplied, and their sin is become exceedingly grievous.

21 I will go down and see whether they have done according to the cry that is come to me: or whether it be not so, that I may know. 22 And they turned themselves from thence, and went their way to Sodom: but Abraham as yet stood before the Lord. 23 And drawing nigh he said: Wilt thou destroy the just with the wicked? 24 If there be fifty just men in the city, shall they perish withal? and wilt thou not spare that place for the sake of the fifty just, if they be therein? 25 Far be it from thee to do this thing, and to slay the just with the wicked, and for the just to be in like case as the wicked, this is not beseeming thee: thou who judges all the earth, wilt not make this judgment.

26 And the Lord said to him: If I find in Sodom fifty just within the city, I will spare the whole place for their sake. 27 And Abraham answered, and said: Seeing I have once begun, I will speak to my Lord, whereas I am dust and ashes. 28 What if there be five less than fifty just persons? wilt thou for five and forty destroy the whole city? And he said: I will not destroy it, if I find five and forty. 29 And again he said to him: But if forty be found there, what wilt thou do? He

said: I will not destroy it for the sake of forty. 30 Lord, said he, be not angry, I beseech thee, if I speak: What if thirty shall be found there? He answered: I will not do it, if I find thirty there.

31 Seeing, said he, I have once begun, I will speak to my Lord. What if twenty be found there? He said: I will not destroy it for the sake of twenty. 32 I beseech thee, said he, be not angry, Lord, if I speak yet once more: What if ten should be found there? And he said: I will not destroy it for the sake of ten. 33 And the Lord departed, after he had left speaking to Abraham: and Abraham returned to his place."

It appears that God was actually quite rational here. He listened to Abraham's questions and respected those questions and answered them in a fair manner. If you continue reading the account, which continues in Genesis chapter 19, Abraham was ultimately trying to save his nephew Lot and family from impending doom because they lived in Sodom which was to be destroyed. God sent two Angels into Sodom and Gomorrah to investigate to see if the outcry was true and they found that only Lot and his family were worthy of being warned and saved. This was discovered by Lot's willingness to help the Angels as the people of the city attempted to violate the Angels. Lot and his family were warned by the Angels about the coming destruction of the cities Sodom and Gomorrah and thus were allowed to flee. But even with explicit instructions, Lot and his wife and daughters did not all make it safely away. As they were fleeing the city and the destruction began, Lot's wife defied the explicit instructions given to them by the Angels and *she* then also lost her life, and of the entire population of the cities, only Lot and his two daughters survived that terrible event.

What we have to realize about these particular stories of annihilation of entire peoples in the Bible is that, these people were **not** innocent and they *substantially* violated the fundamental natural laws of decency and respect towards their fellow man–laws that were established by God.

If there are no parameters by which we must abide, then we can all do whatever we want to do to anyone who we want to do it to at any time we choose to do it. That means that if someone wants to rob and then kill you then they are allowed to do so without penalty. Is this good? Is this just? What is the point of law without any penalty or punishment? What is the point of law if the rules of law change with the winds of society?

The natural laws of God are obvious to those who follow and understand Truth, but since so many of us seem unable to grasp the fundamental concept of *Truth*, God eventually had to compose a list of the obvious natural laws in the form of the Ten Commandments. The Ten Commandments are essentially guidelines of mutual respect towards God and our fellow man by which **all** *of humankind* is to abide. And "God's people", the Israelites, were tasked with sharing that information with *all* of the inhabitants of Earth.

"Morality" **is** these natural laws, and they don't change–ever! The natural laws are simply laws that forbid *unjust* destruction and *unjust* disrespect, and they are violated when we disrespect those who are Created in the image of God. These natural laws of respect not only bar us from harming others, but they also contribute to the building up of others.

Spiritual type stories are interwoven within every part of the Bible. And to be clear, they are interwoven into every part of our lives and *cannot* be avoided. *Spiritual* stories can only be *proven* through using basic human logic, which is part of being "Created in the image of".

There is no one on this Earth who does not understand these fundamental natural laws. Even newborn babies grasp the concept of hurt or the feel of distress. We might choose, as we age, to ignore these natural laws that are the result of Creation and proceed to deny that they exist. Yet we will scream and shout in our public protests that this is not so as a way to distract from our own violations of these natural laws. But that does not change them, the laws are natural and will stand until there is no more nature.

If we mentally strip God out of these natural laws, then the laws still stand, but then there is no enforcer of those laws in our own mind, and thus the illusion of no penalty for violating them.

Some violation of these laws brings on immediate vindication against the violator, but some violations of these laws can persist for a long time if the rest of humanity succumbs to the demands of the violators. When immediate vindication does not occur, it allows for us to continue in our own self-deception regarding these laws. If there is no God, then we can rationalize that no one is being hurt through the violation of these natural laws that are embodied in the Ten Commandments. But is it true that no one is being hurt when we violate those laws?

For those communities that accept violating-behavior as "normal", thus making it socially "moral", the continued violation is certain to bring eventual destruction. When we allow such violations of the explicit instructions contained in the Ten Commandments of God's natural laws, then, we are condoning those violating behaviors that go against God's instruction.

This is where *sin* enters our lives and we are separated from God. The promised "Savior" also acts as our redeemer of our violations of God's natural laws. *Sin* is not tangible, *morality* is not tangible, *Spirit* is not tangible, and *God* is not tangible, which makes it difficult for some of us to relate to all of these intangible concepts. The *results* of violating the natural laws of the Ten Commandments typically are tangible and, for good or for bad, they invoked and defined the *Provable documentable events* recorded in the Bible. Our choice of whether or not to believe and accept this does not change what is true in this regard.

Chapter 12

Let the Words Be Your Guide

Words can be a bit of a complex topic. Words mean things but they can take on a somewhat different meaning than they were originally intended to. We humans think in *lesser* and *greater* concepts, and those concepts are shared with others using words. Words can pack a great deal of information that can go far beyond the basic meanings given in a dictionary. The worst deviations are the perversions of words that have been abused in our modern society, where at the whim of a person using a word as an inappropriate analogy, that word then quickly inherits a new meaning that has no true relevance whatsoever to its original meaning as it is spread throughout the world in a matter of days–We will soon regret that particular rapid fouling of language.

When words take on a somewhat different meaning in typical *normal* conversations, they allow for us to use them as indicators and to accentuate the meaning of a thought, and yet in doing so, they still retain their original meaning but with added information due to the way the word was used.

Biblical Contradictions

When you jump into studying the Bible and begin to read people's books about the Bible or discuss the Bible with others, those who are opponents of the Bible often site supposed contradictions that exist in the Bible in effort to discredit it. It is true that some contradictions do exist in the Bible, but they are few if you really understand the Bible's text.

Perhaps the most notable reason contradiction is found in the Bible's text is our misplaced focus. Consider that if you are taught that two plus two equals five, you will have a difficult time balancing your finances. But if I can convince you that two plus two equals four, then your finances will make more sense and will be accurate. It is no different with the Bible. There are many erred teachings about the Bible, things such as what constitutes a "Jew", or what religion Noah or Moses were. Think about it.

When we have misdirected understanding, it causes us to draw micro conclusions about a particular aspect of the Bible, and that in turn causes us to conclude that there are more contradictions than there actually are. This is a very common problem for many people who work to discredit the Bible.

There is one area of claimed contradiction that is particularly bold where it is suggested that the Bible indicates that God does not change his mind, but then God is talked out of destroying a city or having mercy on someone. This particular misunderstanding is derived from both bad translations and our own misunderstanding. The Bible clearly indicates that *God* does not change; however, this has nothing to do with God having a change of heart towards someone or towards a group of people.

To get a better grasp on this, let's consider Government that likes to change tax laws every several years for no good reason. If we had a truly honest government then the laws would be made once and would stay. Then if someone violated those laws, they might be granted mercy from the court if they are truly repentant and make restitution. But in reality, these laws change often. The Creator, on the other hand, is consistent. Take a look at the Ten Commandments; there is no indication anywhere that they have changed. But if we breach any of the Ten Commandments God will have mercy on us only when we repent of our errors. As you can see, it is easy to take an "unchanging God" and assign to that God an inflexible nature, but this is simply not true or logical. Some folks will continue on this line of thinking and say that when Christ came that He invalidated the Old Testament, and thus The Ten Commandments and all of the other Commands laid down in Exodus and Leviticus are no longer valid, and thus God is not unchanging. But Christ indicated otherwise in no uncertain terms in Matthew chapter five when he said that "For amen I say unto you, till heaven and earth pass, one jot, or one tittle shall not pass of the law, till all be fulfilled." That's a reasonably certain statement that God's laws have not changed and are still in force.

Discrediting the Bible

If you are studying the Bible and believe it to be true, you might find it irritating that anyone would ever attempt to discredit the Bible—but I would like to challenge that notion. There are two classic types of Bible believers; one is based upon blind faith, and nothing will detour them from their belief. Then there are those who approach Bible study a bit more scientifically and are also avid believers.

Those who attempt to discredit the Bible are needed by those who approach it scientifically. This scientific dance of wits is critical for self-checking. Now, I understand that both sides of the debate will vigorously defend their own position and often not back down. Sometimes this is good because they might actually have a valid point worth examining. However, we run into a problem when fact meets fiction. If you must ignore facts to make your point, then you have a problem in your understanding. This then leads us to the problem of "Fact"; what is it?

"Fact" is an interesting subject. What is a fact? Some people say a fact is what is true, and that is a fair enough description. But even though we can have a list of "undeniable facts", it does not mean that we are applying those facts accurately. Take for instance "pagan traditions". It is often claimed that pagan traditions were emulated, but modified, by Christians in effort to get pagans to come into Christianity, and some people believe that Christianity stemmed from paganism. This may be true, but since most pagan traditions, as far as we can tell are from the first few centuries B.C. and after into more recent centuries, it is far more likely that the so-called pagan traditions were derived from the people written of in the Bible, that is to say the Israelites, or Jews as they are often mistakenly called. The Israelite history far predates any pagan traditions that Christianity is sometimes said to have been derived from. Because the Israelite tradition stems from Noah and Shem and Abraham and Isaac, it also predates Egyptian paganism.

The Bible was written as a rolling history and was generally written as that history was occurring. When the Israelites dispersed during and after their captivity, they took with them their traditions. And because those traditions where no longer centralized through the Levite priests, the traditions likely lost a great deal of accuracy and did potentially co-mingle with pagan societies. Regardless, the Israelites were a very influential group, so it is more likely that the pagans blended the Israelites' traditions with their own and that is why we see the similarities in the pagan stories.

In addition to that, some of what we see as pagan tradition could also be poorly passed down Israelite traditions, sort of like the telephone game where you whisper something to one person and they pass it on by whispering it to others until it passes through several people and comes back to the originator somewhat different, and when doing this with pagans the pagans will inadvertently insert their pagan understanding to assist in relaying the message as best they are able. The important purpose of the Bible is the *accurate* passing on of that information, but not every Israelite group had access to the books that we now find in the Bible, and thus they would have had to attempt to pass some of the key things on down to their children verbally, from memory, after they dispersed into other cultures.

Revelation of Words

When we learn how to understand words, then those words can reveal more information than we see on the surface while we read. In saying this, I am not talking about some secret hidden information that people pretend exists in the Bible. I am talking about the information that sits in plain site that we fail to see because of our prejudices and our lack of understanding language and the words that make up that language.

When translating text from language to language, we could simply find the new language's match on a word-for-word basis. But if we did so, then many translated sentences would simply not make any sense to the people who speak the language that the Bible text was being translated into. So when text is translated, we are more concerned about the concepts in each collective thought, rather than the meaning of each specific word. The goal of a qualified translator is to convey the *lesser* and *greater* concepts of the thought that was originally intended or conveyed in the words originally used. This means that the translators need to have a very comprehensive view of both the origin language and of the subject matter. This is especially true when there is no specific word in the *new language* to represent the thought or concept of a specific word in the *original language*. It is at this point that a translator's knowledge and their understanding of that knowledge become invaluable tools in the translation process.

In a previous chapter we discussed some of these translation issues, but we didn't dive far into this aspect. Understanding what was occurring, as described in the text of the Bible, allows for the translator to more clearly reveal the events that occurred and the sentiments involved in the events. The word "reveal" means to pull the curtain back or *re-veil*. The "re" part means to go back or to start again. That is why we say **re**-run when watching movies over again, because we go back to the beginning so that we can **re**-run the movie. So, to *reveal* is to *re-veil*, and that means to pull the veil open or back. When we pull back the veil it allows us to see things that we otherwise would miss.

Unfortunately, when we think of *un*veiling something, we make the improper assumption that the "something" was *intended* to be hidden by a curtain or veil. In fact, regarding the Old Testament, there were Jewish rabbis and mystics who were able to explain deeper understanding of the Bible's Old Testament text. But the Jewish rabbis and mystics of the time had inside information that allowed them to know things about the text that most people were not aware of. And since the idea of mass production of the Bible was *not* an option two-thousand plus years ago, the rest of the people could not study the text on their own because they could not go to a book store to buy a Bible for twenty dollars because Bibles, or scripture, was only in the hands of the leaders. Reproduction of the text was very time consuming to do accurately, so only the priests had that information. This forced the people to rely only on the rabbis and mystics and priests for interpretation of the text or to somehow get access to read or hear the text. Those same rabbis, mystics, and priests would likely not stand out in the same way today, because in our modern culture *everyone* can read and scrutinize the text of the Bible to reveal the so-called "hidden" things.

So, when we see that things in the Bible need to be, or can be, "revealed", or **re-veil**ed, what we need to ask ourselves is, what are they being hidden by? What is this "veil" or curtain that needs to be pulled back? When something is "revealed" to us in the text of the Bible, what we have to understand is that nothing in the text changed, but something in our mind or in our thinking did change. And it is that change or the source or need for it that is the veil that hides what has always been in plain view for all to see all along. What is it that is in our mind or thinking that inhibits our ability to see these so-called "hidden" things? Or more succinctly put, why is our mind hiding the finer details of the Bible's text?

The Bible is *not* some mystical book that all of us are incapable of understanding. *Everyone* has the ability to read and understand the Bible provided that they are open to doing so. Sadly, there are very few of us who are open enough or willing to forego our current belief system that we have invested so much of our being in. Our *veil* of fog is often more than one thing, but those things always culminate in the form of our one-track minds that disregard any thought that doesn't fit our presuppositions.

How to Look

When we understand *how* to look for things, they tend to show themselves more readily. People who have things regularly revealed to them from the Bible are not some sort of mystical people who alone possess the power to interpret the Bible. Anyone can do it provided they are ready, willing, and able to shed their previous belief system when needed, and then seek *only* Truth.

For a lot of us, the thought of forfeiting our current belief system frightens us because we have put so much of our reputation and being into that belief system to a point where it has become our identity as spoken of in the book *Hot Water*. I am not suggesting that it is wrong that our belief system is our identity. But rather, if we have the *wrong* belief system, then our identity is very fragile and can be easily dismantled by anyone who has the ambition to do so. If you feel threatened by considering other religious perspectives, then there is certainly something in your belief system that leaves you feeling vulnerable. If your belief system is built upon Truth, then it should be unshakable and should be able to stand up against *all* scrutiny. But when our belief system is built on blind-faith alone, then we fear to test it because we fear losing *self* and the identity of that *self*. Then when we are pressed for answers, we become angry at our inquisitors because we lack the answers that they seek.

When *Truth* is our guide, things in the Bible become apparent and we tend to do more listening and analyzing than we do talking and indoctrinating. Approaching the Bible with the crystal-clear lenses of Truth causes the text of the Bible to bring forth many things that will then seem very obviously apparent to you. The information that the text of the Bible bears is abundant and tends to have a cascading effect. The cascade effect begins when one thing becomes apparent and frees your mind enough to a point where another thing then becomes apparent, and this tends to continue from one thing previously hidden by your mind to the next thing previously hidden by your mind. But when we choose to believe things that are not exactly correct, it quickly slams that veil tightly shut.

Our task as humans is now, always has been, and will always be to stay on the path of Truth. We are instructed to do so in the Bible. Thus if you fail to stay on the path of Truth, then you are not following the Bible. This puts us in a bit of a difficult position because when we study the Bible, we think that we are doing things properly. Yet, if you follow a path that is not exactly true, then you get caught in those errors and are then no longer able to see the next thing that your mind is hiding from you, and then the floodgate that causes the cascade of information, quickly slams tightly shut.

Chapter 13

Language is Fluid, Historical Events are Not

The last chapter discussed the fact that the meaning of words can change. And in our modern era of technology, such changes can occur in a matter of days. This does not replace the actual original meaning of the word, but over time, the meaning can change in the minds of those who use the word improperly. This is why language is considered to be "fluid". The fluidity of language increases when we translate text from one language to the next due to the fluidity of the words used in the translation. This complicates the understanding process for the people who read the now newly-translated text.

Replication

The purpose of translation is more than just changing the language. It also includes replicating the events or sentiments conveyed in the original text, and then trying to embody that replication in the new language. Replication of the events or sentiments is the goal of any true translator. Without good translation, the meaning of the text can vary from one Bible version to the next, which tells us that the text is fluid and can be interpreted differently from version to version. This is not the goal of good translators or anyone who truly cares about textual accuracy. The Biblical text was rigid and was never intended to be altered. It told a story, and the authors wanted that information able to be passed on for historical documentation purposes to subsequent generations, otherwise there simply is no point in writing it down.

Abundance of Versions

Because language is fluid and is able to change through word definition and through translation, we need to take extra care when trying to understand the text. But while text and translations are fluid, history is not.

History is a hard set of events that occurred, and those events cannot be altered. So if our understanding of that history is incorrect or inaccurate, the history itself still remains constant. The error in our own understanding of that history is our own problem. The facts are available for us to review, but depending upon our biases, and willingness to consider all of the events, our perspective can be greatly altered so as to *not* align with the actual history.

Let's take, for instance, wars—which side is right? Sometimes it is obvious to outsiders which country is the violator, but often it is a matter of perspective. If you consider the Israel-Muslim conflicts that have been plaguing the world for a very long time, you will see this issue of *perspective* in plain sight. Both Israel and the Palestinians see the land of Israel/Palestine as theirs. Both sides in the conflict have a belief that God bestowed the land to them. Who is right? And who is wrong? Mohammed was instructed to tell idolaters, along with Jews and Christians that had fallen away from God, to return to true faith, which has nothing to do with the land of Israel/Palestine, and Mohammed came along many centuries after the land was given to Abraham, with some of it later being specifically designated for the Israelites.

As you can see, when we read our Holy Books, we tend to interpret them the way *we* want them to be interpreted, or the way we were taught to interpret them. It is only when we remove our preconceptions that cloud our view of the text that we can more clearly see what it all says, and what it actually means.

When it comes to translation and the interpretation of the translations, some words that are seemingly insignificant can greatly change the meaning or intensity of a sentence. Words like "and" or "the" or "if" can sometimes be replaced with other words potentially altering meaning, but that is usually not a problem. Other words such as "earth" or "heaven" are always interpreted from our human perspective, but not all usages of those two words are what we understand them to be; it is a chicken-versus-egg understanding issue as is explained in *The Science Of God Volume one – The First Four Days.*

Fornication

Due to language fluidity, there are other words that we typically understand incorrectly that might involve something in particular, but are really not about what they might involve. The most notable of such words is "fornication". We often think of fornication as intimate relations between those who are not married. But if you have known someone in that way you then technically have married them in a biblical sense, and then to further partake in such activity with others makes you an adulterer rather than a fornicator. That is one of the many reasons why we require Salvation. This classic interpretation error is prevalent in our Christian understanding, as well as for non-Christian believers, such as Jews. Fornication is not about sex, but it often does involve such activities. Fornication appears at times to have involved some form of sex, but that was not in itself fornication. Fornication has to do with not serving God and making offerings or placing our admiration and dependency on anything other than God and at the same time asking for sustenance from that which we admire. God's people often fornicated with other nations as a whole. Fornication is also when offerings that would normally have gone to God went to other false gods. And the worst case of fornication had to do with human sacrifice and children, details of which we won't discuss in this book, and none of which ever went well for the fornicators.

Because of the fluidity of language, we have difficulty today fully interpreting terms such as "fornication". The Bible text discussing fornication indicates that it generally always involves idolatry and sometimes also involved human sacrifice, or objects and food sacrificed to idols, or placing affection towards other countries or kings instead of God, but often it also includes sexuality. We mistakenly miss the other atrocities that are described in the Bible under the label of "fornication". Fornication is far more heinous than is basic adultery. The reason we misunderstand fornication is due to the fact that we were instructed to *not* partake in it and thus, in our modern era, we are not familiar with it in our culture, but as of the early twenty-first century it appears to be making a comeback. People generally do not do human sacrifice, although, that is partly what abortion actually is. The incorrect interpretation of fornication comes mostly from Saul-Paul's epistle writings about it because it is mentioned adjacent to adultery in his text.

As you can see, language fluidity causes almost every one of us to struggle to properly and fully understand the text of the Bible. Think about it.

Chapter 14

The History of the Lives of a People

In our era today, we hear of Middle-East conflict on a near daily basis, but few of us understand these conflicts. We have a difficult time understanding the conflicts because we are not familiar with the history, which goes back–way back. Many wars today are thug-wars where some rogue leader comes to power and oppresses the people of that country. Then the people or the neighboring countries will step in to stop the oppression which sometime causes the rogue leader to prevail over his foes and fight against those who are trying to stop him. Wars like this typically are short-lived, usually only lasting a matter of months or a few years, or sometimes they will last until the death of the rogue leader, which can be several decades of rogue rule. If the people within the country fail to rise up and overthrow the rogue leader, then subsequent generations learn to submit to that rogue-style oppression and never seem to be able to come out of it because they have learned to continually submit to that rogue leader.

The Israel-Muslin conflict is different and it is multifaceted, and it is old. Without getting too detailed here, it is more than just the Muslims fighting the Jews, and it cannot be understood without understanding the Bible and knowing some Biblical history.

This is another point where we need to apply mental separation. When you achieve this particular mental separation, you will begin to see the real historical need for understanding the Bible. The Bible is not just a book about Salvation, it is also a history book of geopolitics that cannot be denied. No one on this Earth, no matter how much they know or try to denounce the Bible as fairytales, can avoid this history or legitimately deny it without looking like a fool, because many of the peoples mentioned in the Bible, especially the old testament, exist to this very day as do the contentions between some of them.

Who are These People Anyway?

As a preface to this section, it must be stated that if you are a Christian who truly understands the Bible, you will not be against Islam. However, neither would you convert to Islam by practice because you already hold the keys to Salvation in your hands in knowing Christ and that the Salvation of all men is bought and brought by The Christ. To cast this aside is to cast aside your Salvation. The sort of "Islam" that is practiced by many Muslims today is different than "Islam" as instructed in the Quran.

To understand the Israel-Muslim conflict we first have to understand how Muslims came about. The word "Muslim" means *one who submits to God*. The word "Islam" means to *submit or surrender to God*. The mental separation here is minor. "Islam" is the *act* of submitting one's self or surrendering to God (or Allah as Muslims put it) and "Muslim" is *the person* who submits. The word *Qur'an*, sometimes spelled "Koran", means *reading*. Often referred to as "Al Qur'an" meaning *The Reading*.

The Muslim religion is often associated with Arabic people because that is, in fact, the area of the globe from which the Muslim religion arose. If you apply another mental separation between "Muslim" and "Arab" you will quickly see that many Arabs are *not* Muslims and many Muslims are *not* Arabs. Islam being a *religion*, is something that anyone can choose to do, or in some cases be forced to do, just as anyone can choose to be a Christian. In conjunction with the preface to this section, it must be pointed out that according to the Adam and Eve account and the reason this concept of Salvation exists to begin with, you can honor and serve God all you want, but if you reject the Savior, then you will *not* be saved. So if a Muslim were to reject Christ, then they would be rejecting their Salvation, even though they might honor God more than a typical Christian does. However, the Muslims do acknowledge Jesus The Christ, but they do it differently than most Christians, which can be problematic for them regarding their Salvation. Now, on with the story!

A little-known piece of information about Muslims is that only about fifteen percent of them are Arabic. So why the deep connection to Arabs? And where did the Muslims come from?

In the seventh century around 610 AD it is believed that a man by the name of Mohammed was visited by, or saw a vison of, the Angel Gabriel. There were several of these encounters which have been written and kept and compiled into what is called "The Reading" or "Al Quran". The Quran is the "Holy Book" of the Muslims, it is their "Bible". But there is a great deal of misunderstanding that most people have about this "Muslim Bible". The first misunderstanding is that it would likely offend them if you called it their "Bible" because to them it is "Al Quran". This would be as confusing and as offensive if a Muslim called your Bible the Christian Quran. But given the meanings of the names of both of these books, either name is somewhat true to the meanings of the actual names of both books.

However, since the Quran mentions the Scriptures and those to whom the Scriptures were given, it is important to keep the mental separation between the Bible and the Quran clearly in mind. If not for the Bible and the historical events that are chronicled within the Bible, the Quran *could not* exist. The Quran is not *instead* of or in place of the Bible, rather it is *after* or *in addition to* the Bible, and it is often misinterpreted by its readers as is the Bible.

An additional important point about the Quran is that the Quran was compiled *after* the death of Mohammed when a request was put out that anything written of Mohammed's words was to be assembled along with verbal accounts of Mohammed's sayings. This initial assembly of the Qur'an was used for a short time. Then as a means of clarification, similar to the Bible being canonized, the Quran was recompiled at one point and all previous copies were to be burned so that only one version would be available for consistent reproduction.

The content of the Quran is **not** made up of *only* words said by the angel Gabriel. Many of the words in the Quran are accounts of events, or are opinions or the sayings of Mohammed that were relayed to the Quran's assembler by acquaintances of Mohammed during its compilation. This is similar to the Bible in that it is **not** all "inspired".

When Mohammed had these visions, he tried to share them with his family, and immediately, all but his wife thought he was a bit crazy. However, after a bit of persistence, his family and friends began to see the value in what he was saying. What often is not discussed regarding Mohammed is that many people of his home area and the surrounding areas were idolaters and they loved their idolatry and worshipping their idols, but there were also good Christians and Jews who were not idolaters in those areas, although some of them did fall away from God.

During Mohammed's encounters with Gabriel, Gabriel instructed Mohammed to inform the people that idolatry was wrong and was offensive to God/Allah. When Mohammed tried to share this with the people, most of them rejected his message and continued in their idolatry. If you wonder about how this might have looked, just consider relatively recent internal conflict all around the globe

As time progressed, Mohammed slowly convinced many people that idolatry was wrong, and as the numbers grew, those who held fast to their idolatry eventually became hostile towards Mohammed and those who heeded his information. This hostility grew until battles arose between Mohammed and his idolatrous opponents... Skipping a great deal of the story here... Mohammed eventually prevailed. Mohammed wanted peaceful conversions of people from serving idols, and for them to be changed over to people who serve God. Mohammed initially only battled with those who battled against him. But this changed after his death.

After Mohammed's death, Abu Bakr was installed as his successor, and then after Abu had died and through much bloodshed and treachery, many caliphs came in rapid succession thereafter, too many to bother listing here. Similar to the kings of Israel, some Islam caliphs were good, but others not-so-good.

What was once strictly for the purpose of informing people about the God and that any idolatry should be abolished, quickly turned to little more than a bloody power-grab and a desire for the spoils of war. If you have read the history of Islam, you know that it is safe to conclude that Mohammed would not have been pleased with much of the atrocities done in the name of "Islam", nor would his visitor, the Angel Gabriel. In fact, the Christian Crusades have, at the end of the twentieth-century, been depicted as some random slaughtering-quest done by Christians. But if you're honest, and you seek to know the truth, then you will acknowledge the part that Islam and certain corrupt caliphs and certain other Muslims played regarding the Crusades in the eleventh through thirteenth centuries.

It is impossible to understand the history of Islam without understanding the people of the Bible and that Mohammed's instruction was to divert people from serving idols and direct them to God/Allah. And while that was occurring, there was also improper imposition of new caliphs' interpretation of the Quran onto peaceful Christians. Islam had overstepped its authority many times since Mohammed has died, and this overstepping still occurs by a few unsavory members of Islam in our modern era. But to be clear, not all Muslims share that unsavory approach or view.

Ishmael

So, why are the Arabs so strongly connected to Mohammed and Islam? This mental separation goes back to the roots of the Arab nations. So, now we're going to back up a bit for the Biblical connection and the invaluable and unavoidable Biblical history that connects all of this.

When Abraham left his idolatrous father, Terah, and went out on his own, he married Sarai. Abraham, whose name was "Abram" at the time, and Sarai his wife had been wanting a child for a long time, but Sarai was not able to conceive. As they traveled abroad, they entered Egypt and through some personal conflicts involving the Egyptian King Abimelech and Abram's wife Sarai, the King, as a token of good faith, gave Abram gifts and a servant girl by the name of Hagar. Abram, Sarai, and Hager then left Egypt and dwelt abroad.

After years of unsuccessful attempts by Sarai to have a child for Abram, Abram was told by God that he eventually would have a son. After waiting and trying to bear a son for Abram with no result, Sarai became impatient and thought up the questionable idea to use Hagar as a surrogate to give Abram the promised child. Abram, agreed and went into Hagar and she conceived and bore a male child for Abram. But before the boy named Ismael was even born, Sarai became displeased with the situation because she believed that Hager despised her after Hagar became pregnant. Sarai's attitude towards Hagar drove

Hagar to run away shortly after the child was born. But when not far off, Hagar was instructed by a messenger from God that she and her child were to return to Abram and Sarai.

Sometime after, Abram was again visited by the Lord and told that Sarai would bear a son for Abram and that there would be a perpetual covenant between Abram and God, and that Abram would be the Father of many nations. Abram was told that he would no longer be known as Abram, but rather, his new name would be "Abraham". And that Sarai would no longer be known as Sarai, but instead was now to be called "Sarah".

Much later, when Abraham and Sarah, Hagar and her son Ishmael lived in the Mambre area, Abraham was visited by three messengers who informed him that Sarah would soon bear a son, but being well advanced in years, Sarah, overhearing the conversation from behind the tent door, laughed at this idea. The messengers asked why she laughed, but she denied doing so.

The reason Sarah had laughed at the thought of her bearing a child is because she was about ninety years old at the time. This visit from these messengers is the very same visit about which Abraham was told of the impending doom of Sodom and Gomorrah. After about a year's time, Sarah did bear a child in her advanced years. Sarah's son was called *Isaac*. After the child, Isaac, was born and had been weaned, Abraham made a great feast on the day of Isaac's weaning. And when Sarah saw Hagar the Egyptian playing with Isaac, she became jealous and demanded that Abraham "Cast out this bondwoman, and her son: for the son of the bondwoman shall not be heir with my son Isaac."

This grieved Abraham, but God instructed him to not let it seem grievous to him regarding the boy and the bondwoman, and that all Sarah had said Abraham should do because it is to be in Isaac that Abraham's seed shall be *called*. God also told Abraham that the son of the bondwoman, Hagar, would also become a great nation because the boy Ishmael was also from the seed of Abraham. So, Abraham got up early the next morning and gave

Hagar some bread and water and sent her away with the teenage boy. Hagar departed and wandered in the wilderness of Bersabee, and when her water supply was gone she had her son sit beneath a tree and she went far off from him because she did not want to see her son die, and she lifted up her voice and wept.

God heard the voice of her son and an angel called to Hagar from Heaven and asked her what she was doing, and said that God has heard the voice of her son and instructed her to take the boy by the hand and that her son would become a great nation. Her eyes were opened and she saw a well and filled her water vessel and her son drank. God was with her son Ishmael, and he grew and dwelt in the wilderness and became an archer. And the Arab nation was born.

From Douay Rheims Genesis Chapter 25: "13 And these are the names of his children according to their calling and generations. The firstborn of Ismael was Nabajoth, then Cedar, and Adbeel, and Mabsam. 14 And Masma, and Duma, and Massa, 15 Hadar, and Thema, and Jethur, and Naphis, and Cedma. 16 These are the sons of Ismael: and these are their names by their castles and towns, twelve princes of their tribes."

Isaac

Sarah's son Isaac was the son of Abraham, whom God had made the covenant with Abraham about. Isaac was to be the son through whom Abraham's seed would be *called*. Isaac had two sons by the names Esau and Jacob. Jacob had twelve sons who are the fathers or patriarchs of the twelve tribes of Israel. Jacob, as discussed in an earlier chapter, was renamed "Israel". The sons of Jacob are Ruben, Simeon, Levi, Juda, Issachar, Zabulon, Joseph, Benjamin, Dan, Nephtali, Gad, and Asher—*They* and their offspring are the Twelve Tribes of Israel, or more commonly known as "the *Israelites*" or "*God's People*".

But Ishmael, the son of Abraham and Hagar, does not disappear from the history books here. **Ishmael** became the father of nations, and it is those nations that are the *Arab* nations of today. When you hear the Arab Muslims refer to God, they will do so by saying the God of *Abraham* and *Ishmael*, where the Israelites speak of the God of *Abraham, Isaac,* and *Jacob*.

This very brief account of the introduction of two of the several nations, *Arabs* and *Israelites*, that descended from Abraham is a very brief account of the already brief account that is discussed in Genesis chapters 15 through 21.

Your awareness of this particular mental separation is crucial to your ability to understand modern geopolitics *and* the Bible. As you read through the Bible, you will come across this particular division often, but few people realize that it exists, and thus, for many people, the Bible is just a bunch of confusing stories of random arbitrary conflicts between random arbitrary peoples. But it is neither random nor arbitrary.

The information in this particular chapter that you are reading cannot be historically denied. However, there are minor issues that people will debate regarding some of the text, such as specific ages of people, but no one debates this basic lineage of the Israelites and Jews, or the lineage of the Ishmaelites who are where the Arabic nations originate from. The New Testament events are well documented, but other than the Old Testament prophecies being fulfilled through the New Testament events and the people's origins, we have not discussed any solid evidence to bring credibility to the Old Testament.

It is the people who descended from Abraham, especially those from Ishmael and Isaac, that stand as a testament to the Old Testament's credibility. If you debate this you are up against about two billion Christians, millions of Jews, and nearly two billion Muslims, of which about a half billion are Arab Muslims. Further, other nations who do not follow the Bible or the Quran, such as China, do not hold much opinion on this topic as they reject God altogether, nor are they qualified to do so because their culture will not freely allow learning about such topics.

This basic history is undisputed and only those who dwell in folly dare to challenge this particular history. And if they do, they are quickly laid low because the historical writings, both Biblical and non-Biblical, and the physical evidence of places and things and people are written all over the region and cannot be avoided or completely erased.

Nearly all of the wars in the Middle-East are centered around these relationships. Those who set out in attempt to prove this to be false always either retreat in defeat or change their perspective of this basic information when they take the time to actually understand it. I challenge anyone on the face of this Earth to prove with even a speck of concrete evidence, or any convincing evidence of antiquity in writing, to prove this to not be true. There may be some minor discrepancies in the historical details, but those minor discrepancies do not nullify the overall and obvious evidence and testimony of many historians with over hundreds and even thousands of years of research and documentation collectively by them all.

Chapter 15

Does the Bible Agree with Itself?

It's a difficult thing to watch both Jews and Christians be crushed by irrational articulation against the events of the Bible, which occurs only because many Jews and Christians do not have the knowledge and understanding that they imagine and profess themselves to have. When challenged by any clever opponent, most Jews, Christians, and even Muslims, cannot withstand the scrutiny of a clever debater because they do not know or understand the information in their own holy books.

I was once given a Quran by a person who I had been doing business with. The book sat for a number of months, when the man eventually asked if I had read it. I answered, "No, not yet", at which point he insisted that I read it as soon as possible. So, to honor his request, I set out to read it. When I completed reading the Quran, I had many questions ready-and-waiting for him to answer.

The man was a first-generation immigrant from Lebanon, whose American name was "Mike". Mike was a Muslim. He would talk with me about Islam and God, or "Goad" as he pronounced it in his broken English, and he would articulate the reasons why Islam is important. We had several conversations about the Quran and the Bible that all occurred *before* he gave me the book. My assumption was that he was somewhat studied in the Quran, so after I had completed reading the copy of the Quran he sent to me, I was quite excited for the opportunity to question him about it and Islam.

When I asked him about it, he began telling me of its importance, and with every word I became more and more excited about being able to get specific answers that would be absent of any American-Christian influence and opinion. When I began asking questions, he rapidly answered them as he was able. Later, as the conversations proceeded, I began asking about very specific points I read in various *Surahs* (Chapters or Books) in the Quran. This is where he started to avoid answering my questions. I wanted to know about some of the things I had read and so I pressed the issue with him on various questions, until at one point he was forced to admit that he had never read the book that he insisted I read. He was taught about it growing up, but had never read it completely, and in fact, he admitted that he read very little of it. He was very familiar with some of it, but he was far more familiar with Islam the religion as told to him by his culture.

Now please understand that this was a kind man whose heart was in the right place, and he believed everything he discussed with me, without question. But his lack of knowledge of the actual text of the Quran barred him from being able to intelligibly discuss its actual contents. Many Christians scoff at this as if he was almost some sort of hypocrite, as if it is a requirement that he should have read his entire holy book, which is really quite brief relative to the Bible. But over the years, I have chatted with many Christians and a few Jews on matters of religion and the Old Testament. Many of these people had quite a good range of knowledge of their respective religions and I enjoyed speaking with them. However, similar to Mike from

Lebanon, when pressed on their views of events in the Bible, they would be evasive in some of their answers. Most of these conversations occurred before or around the same time that I met Lebanon-Mike. After my encounter with Mike and the revelation that he never read his entire holy book, I realized that the same was likely true of the Jews and Christians that I had the opportunity to speak with. So of those with whom I still had regular contact, I asked them if they had ever read the Bible. To which of course the answer was "Yes" from every one of them.

I pressed the issue of having read the Bible a bit further and asked if they ever read the *whole* Bible, to which every one of them answered "yes" or "probably". The reason that someone would not know for sure and would even think to answer "probably" is because many, if not most Christians, start reading the Bible in the New Testament and then when prompted by questions that arise, they will then proceed to search in the Old Testament and find the answer that they are looking for, or they have some other reason to read a few verses from the Old Testament. Many people will read much of Bible, but never really know for sure if they have read all of it.

To press the point a bit further, I went on to ask every one of these people if they had ever read the Bible from cover to cover from front to back and the answer was an overwhelming "No", with the exception of maybe one or two people. Why am I bringing people's reading habits up in a book about the Bible? Two reasons:

Cross-Referential Support

The first reason I bring up people's Bible reading habits is because the order of reading is a fairly clear indicator that many questions that arise when a person reads the Bible in a broken manner, can be answered from other parts of the Bible. This illustrates that when you look at the prophecies and the historical events and the mention of peoples that you see later in the Bible, that in order to understand those events, you need to find the context in earlier books of the Bible–that is to say the Old Testament of the Bible. But this does not prove that the Bible is true.

What it does prove is that the Bible is a reasonably consistent continuous record of history that proves itself to all be connected. The documents in the Bible are not some random stack of writings that someone decided should be bound into a book and called "The Bible". They are writings that are specific in that they follow the people of Abraham via Isaac and Jacob through which the covenant with Abraham regarding his seed would continue.

In this, the Bible agrees in reasonable harmony with itself. However, if you seek them out there are a few discrepancies that defy the "inerrant" status often given to the Bible by many blind-faithed believers. This incorrect view of inerrancy overshadows the actual true history of the Bible and causes many unwitting people to turn away, because when you find these inconsistencies, it proves that the Bible is not "inerrant" in that person's mind. But had they not been taught this myth of inerrancy they would likely not have turned from the Bible or its information because their view of the Bible would then be more logical.

The Bible, overall, is quite consistent, but the translations are not perfect because there are anomalies in the translations. The question is: Are these the fault of the original Hebrew, Aramaic, Greek, and Latin text copies? Or are they possibly the fault of the translators as well as the nuances of translation and the languages that the text is translated *from* and *to*? Is it also further possible that the anomalies have to do with our own understanding and interpretation of the text? Yes, yes, and yes to those questions.

The reality is that it is likely all three points. The original Hebrew, Aramaic, and Greek text copies have been carried through the exile period of the Israelites and the later exile of the Jews, and some of the books or documents that were carried along with them had been translated to another language in the pre-Christ era. It is very possible that some of those anomalies occurred during the exile translation, and have mostly to do with specifics of ages and order of events, such as genealogies, etc. But none of those have any substantial effect on the overall history described in the Bible. Nor do they alter the reason that these texts had been carried through the years and compiled as they are.

Many of these anomalies have to do with the translation efforts and the way in which the translators understood the text. For instance, if you are a child and taught all your life that Hagar was sent away with a very young child near to an infant's age and you are tasked with translating the Bible or interpreting it, it is likely that in the language you use in describing the details of Hagar being sent away at the request of Sarah, you might confuse that with when Hagar ran away shortly after the birth of Ishmael and thus Ismael's real age is not properly projected in some people's understanding of that particular point. I will leave it to you to do the math on that, but it is these sorts of translation problems and claims of "inerrancy" that cause people to get confused, and then when they are unable to continue in their inerrancy rouse, they turn from both the Bible *and* from God.

We Don't Read, We Don't Know

The other reason that I bring up people's Bible reading habits beside the cross-referential consistency issues mentioned in the last section, is because we typically don't know. What is it that we don't know? A lot!

One important point about the Quran is that you truly cannot understand it if you have never read the Bible cover to cover. Without the Biblical events, the Quran **could not** exist. Any "Christian" who reads the Quran and then converts to Islam without having read the Bible cover to cover is choosing very foolishly.

Much like Lebanon-Mike, we are taught all about the basics, such as the stories in a Children's Bible. Please note here that I am not discrediting children's Bibles, in fact, I encourage Mom's and Dad's to sit with your children on your lap and read those stories to your children or grandchildren. Teach your children to read, and encourage them to read those stories on their own as they age, but don't stop teaching them. As we grow older, we somehow imagine that we have "read the Bible". But the Children's Bible doesn't really count when it comes to Bible study and adult-Bible reading and understanding.

Earlier it was mentioned that most people read the Bible in a somewhat random manner because Christians often start reading the Bible by reading the New Testament first. Then, when questions arise, we need to look things up in the Old Testament to get a bit of context of what we read in the New Testament. This is not wrong, but it does present a problem that has arisen many times in discussions I had with people regarding Biblical topics. As we read the New Testament and then seek answers in the Old Testament, more often than not we fail in our quest and instead we turn to books that are not the Bible, *written by people, about the questions* that arise. Then, when we start to read people's books about the Bible, and there are many, we begin a journey down a road of *opinion* that has no end. At this point, our attention turns to opinions that sooth our itching ears, causing the Bible to fade from our view. This causes our quest to be more about our own beliefs and our own opinions about the Bible, rather than having our quest be the Bible's true text and better understanding that text.

The reason that this is so prevalent in Christianity is because we are somewhat lazy, and we hear only those things that we want to hear, making us feel righteous, thus espousing our virtue to the world. Another reason this is so prevalent is that we have not read the Bible cover to cover to try to see what **God** has to say. Too often we invent false religious laws that *do not exist* in the Bible, and then we wrongly ascribe that false doctrine to the

Bible and to God. To do so is to be a liar and a false preacher. This problem is discussed further in the book *Understanding The Church*.

When this occurs, it is common for us to claim that our belief is written "between the lines" when nothing could be further from the truth. Our self-righteous ways are not helpful to ourselves or to others when we follow errors, or "half-truths", or the lies of others, or when we invent our own inaccurate doctrine. The text is explicit and it doesn't change. We must stop trying to alter it to fit our habits and preferred beliefs. If you want to drill down to the truth, then cast away all preconceptions and re-open your Bible on *page **one*** and read it until you have finished every page in numerical order before attempting to teach others with misperceived or erred doctrine that someone else or you may have found "between the lines." ***Do not be a false preacher!***

Chapter 16

Finding the Messages Between the Lines

Are there messages that hide between the lines of the Bible as some people claim there are? If there are, then can those messages be extracted to teach us *all* deeper meanings? The answers to these questions depend upon your honesty and who you follow. Do you follow priests, popes, and preachers, or do you follow God, Prophets, and Christ?

We have a real problem in Christianity that has been hindering people from feeling welcomed to the Bible, which in turn has hindered them from reading it. This hindrance occurs when we follow the wrong shepherds and ignore the "Good Shepherd". This problem is occurring throughout Christianity and Judaism today and has been occurring for a very long time. It is the main reason that the Reformation took place. And it's all caused by our choice of who we follow and how those we follow choose to read the Bible and what *they* find between the lines. This problem is not exclusive to Christians; it plagues the Jews and the Muslims as well.

The Wrong Messages Between the Lines

Many Christians place more trust in their *priests, popes,* and *preachers,* than they do in *God, Prophets,* and *Christ,* and when these those particular shepherds read between the lines of the Bible, they can arrive at some very wrong ideas as to what *they* interpret the text to say or mean. How can we test *their* interpretation-proposals that are taught as if those proposals are "factual"? And how do they arrive at some of these outlandish beliefs or conclusions?

All of us are susceptible to allowing our emotions and our desires to dictate our interpretation of the Bible. We add things when we need them, and we ignore things when we don't like them. What we seldom see are people who don't manipulate the text for self-serving purposes. In a previous chapter discussing the various approaches that people have when reading the Bible, it was mentioned that we often read the Bible starting with the New Testament and then seek out clarification and context for it from the Old Testament. There is nothing specifically wrong with this approach, but it can be risky for us.

It's very common for us to stumble upon a preacher, or priest who we see on TV or who wrote a book. This person could be still alive today or they could have written a book many years in the past. We typically come across these sources when we're searching either for Biblical information or emotional reprieve. When we find a good honest person, it's usually very beneficial to our quest. However, what all too often occurs is that we find a person who might truly believe that they are being honest, but they take liberties with the interpretation of the Bible, and in doing so they invent rules for people that are simply not in the Bible. These rules are manmade and are despised by God. They are not authorized rules, and they harm the people who follow and believe them to be God's Rules—but they are not **God's** rules—they are man's rules.

This was a very sore spot between the Pharisees and Jesus The Christ, and it led to Jesus' Crucifixion. There is a set of legalistic books referred to as the "Talmud" that dissects the contents of the Bible as if it is court records of legal matters. This is something that has been going on for many years. The Talmud in particular is over 20 volumes of this sort of legalistic nonsense. It's not all wrong, but too much of it steps far beyond its jurisdiction and far beyond the actual words in the Bible. As a sort of beat-all escape from having to answer for rules that step beyond scripture, the idea of "oral tradition" is invoked, thus barring those who are not "learned scholars" from being able to understand the Scriptures. Because most people have not read the Talmud or any part of it, and most people don't even know that it exists they, obviously will not understand it.

Jesus was infuriated by the Scribes and Pharisees. He called them a "brood of vipers" and "hypocrites". They imposed their own interpretation of the Scriptures onto the people and walked about the city in constant judgement of the people, when they themselves would not even follow some of their own man-made rules. These sorts of man-made rules do have some basis in Scripture, but through clever discourse, the Scriptures have been mentally altered by them as they arrogantly imposed their own version of the "law" onto the people.

This still goes on today whether it is through the Talmud's age-old legalistic nonsense, or through some modern or recent centuries priests, popes, or preachers. The Talmud is many thousands of pages of argument of things such as what specifically is considered "work" on the Sabbath. Getting into hair-splitting nonsense that God never intended, such as if I hand you a glass of water through the window, then I am doing "work", but if you were to reach into the window and grab the glass of water I prepared and left sitting on the counter, then that is not work on my part so that would be okay for me, but not you. These are the sort of things that the Scribes, Pharisees, and

Rabbis wrote into the Talmud, none of which is authoritative regarding the Bible. And this still continues to this day.

In our modern day, we have similar things such as priests' or popes' opinions on basic birth control used by married couples consisting of a man and woman. This is something that is *not* in the Bible, but has wrongly been imposed on *married* couples for a long time, making them feel guilty for living their lives as they see fit within the faithful couple, all while some of the church leaders are practicing activities that are punishable by death according to the Bible. This is exactly what the Pharisees did and it was not well received by the Christ who is said to be The Word that was sent by God.

Over twenty volumes, and growing, of legal text is a whole lot of reading between the lines of the Bible for things that simply *do not* exist. Be cautious in who you follow, because they can foul your family and your life, imposing guilt on you that God **never** intended, further causing you to overlook or ignore the actual laws that God *did* command in the Bible. The Bible is a very clear book when you follow Truth and the words of God–and that is when you will find the real messages "between the lines".

Hidden in Plain Sight Between the Lines

We can all quickly learn to **see** if we stop following the wrong shepherds. To begin to see, follow the simple process of reading the *entire* Bible from front to back one page at a time in proper order of page numbers. When we jump around in the Bible without ever having read it in page-order, it allows us to cut out what we don't like, but then paste only the things that we do like into our minds, allowing us to form our own legalistic laws that eventually drive people apart and us away from God. The text will speak for itself when we allow it to do so, but when we decide to speak for the text, we then step into a point of violation of the Bible, of God, of our fellow man, and of ourselves. There certainly is a feeling of things being written between the lines of the Bible, but that is only because we have blinded ourselves with our current beliefs and desires.

If we really want to *see*, then we need to actually try to look *with open eyes of our own*, rather than only looking through other people's eyes. When we learn the skill of recognizing mental separations, then this is probably the first place to put mental separations into practice. Looking through the eyes of others when reading the Bible basically means that we read and obey what *they* believe the Bible says, and then we ignore what we read that opposes our false teachers as we skip over details because we have not read the Bible cover-to-cover ourselves.

It is when we cast away the laws of man and adopt the laws of God that we can begin to read the Bible through the crystal-clear lenses of Truth. This cannot be achieved when we hear and obey priests, popes, and preachers when at the same time we ignore God. This does not mean that everything that they say is wrong, but it does mean that we must follow God, the Bible, the Prophets, and Jesus The Christ rather than following the arbitrary rules of man.

Adopting a God-Prophets-and-Jesus-first approach when studying and reading the Bible will quickly clear your mind of the unneeded and unwanted clutter that God never intended for us to encounter. The information is really not hidden *between* any lines; it is now and always has been out in the open for all to see. However, it is veiled by our reckless blind-faith priests-popes-and-preachers-first approach. There are both good and bad people in those positions, so be cautious of who you choose to follow.

When you start to read the Bible through the Crystal-clear lenses of Truth and read it in page order, cover-to-cover, without your own or someone else's presupposed agenda, then you will likely begin to quickly see the difference between a priests-popes-and-preachers-first approach, versus a God-Prophets-and-Jesus-first approach.

When we use a God-Prophets-and-Jesus-first approach, it is easier to recognize that there is not any hidden information residing between the lines of *any* text in the Bible. It's all out in the open and always has been, and it is *not* a mystery to those who have Truth. But we believe that there is information hidden between the lines because of our veil that needs to be pulled back. Our needlessly blinded-eyes will see any unique revelation that we find as if that information was "hidden between the lines". As we extract pieces of information, those little morsels of information advance our understanding, but they are mysterious to us because they sat in front of our eyes as we read the text for years, while overlooking the context. For some reason, when something clicks in our head and we don't fully understand it, we attribute it to our hidden-between-the-lines logic.

When we open our eyes and pull back the veil and follow God, Prophets, and Jesus Christ first, *that* is when our floodgates of understand begin to open.

Mental separations are important, but there is a point of too much separation. When separation leads to division and discord between people, then we need to re-evaluate our thinking. Taking roughly 1000 pages of Old Testament text and creating 20 plus volumes of hair-splitting human-made legal discourse, as in the Talmud, can be counterproductive. Very little of the Bible is about new rules and laws, so for us to add to those with our own human deviation from those relatively few rules listed in the Bible, is to be ignorant of God's ways as described in the Bible.

Chapter 17

Scripture – What is It?

What is "Scripture"? "Script" is to *scribe* which means to *scratch*, much the way some ancient documents were carved into stone. Very early in human history, things were recorded in some manner, either through carving and scratching or through some form of a coloring used on a surface to draw symbols, all of which uses some form of scratching.

In the New Testament, it speaks of the "scribes" and the Pharisees. The "scribes" were people who inscribed words onto paper or papyrus sheets. Some scribes might have only been writing for others as they took dictation from them, but most were likely what we today would call authors, writers, or reporters. If the "scribes" did not have their own words available for others to read, it is unlikely that Jesus would have said "whoa to you *Scribes* and Pharisees, you hypocrites..."

The Scribes and Pharisees spoke of the "scriptures". The Christ also spoke of the "Scriptures" with reverence and obedience and said, "Do not think that I am come to destroy the law, or the prophets. I am <u>not</u> come to destroy, <u>but to fulfill</u>." But the Scribes and

Pharisees had their own interpretation of the already stated Law that was written in the Scriptures long before. The Law is one of the most important aspects of the "Scriptures" or what we today call the Old Testament.

Prophets

The "Scriptures", or writings, were not intended to be argued over by Scribes and Pharisees, they were intended to document what happened and what was said so that it could be retained and shared with future generations. Otherwise, what's the point of writing those sorts of events down to begin with?

Prophecies being written does not prove that such prophecies had not been written *after* the fact and interwoven in the text as some sort of deception. However, when you consider the complexities of intermingling a detailed prophecy into text that is dependent upon those prophecies—makes it highly unlikely. This is especially true because the prophesied events that occurred often referenced the prophecies and the prophets.

When the prophets were asked to relay messages, they were sometimes told to relay those messages to the people with their own lips, or to remember what they saw or heard, or they were told to "*Write these things down.*" The purpose of writing things down and sharing it with others works as a means of testimony by creating many witnesses as to what had been foretold and written to have been clearly known *in advance* by *many* people. This is historically testified to in parts of the Bible that are subsequent to the prophecies.

When discussing prophecies and their viability and inclusion in what would have been subsequent events, we must be careful to not trap ourselves in circular reasoning. Circular reasoning is used by people who manipulate the Bible's text for their own purpose or gain. This is often done with the Pauline epistles that are found in the New Testament when preachers of today want to believe certain things so they will use circular reasoning to "prove" their point. We also find this deceptive practice in such ideas as big bang theology where the big bang allows the laws of physics and the laws of physics allow the big bang. Yet the laws of physics are said to have *not yet existed* until micro moments after the big bang occurred, which requires the laws of physics to begin with, this is discussed in *The Science Of God – The First Four Days* and in *Bending the Ruler*.

The prophecies are very different because they are linear and are *not* circular in reasoning or in writing. While the subsequent books do speak of the prophecies as an intricate part of the history that was being recorded at the time, the prophecies do *not* need the subsequent events to have occurred. The prophecies have been stated and that was the end of any particular prophecy, no more interaction was required. Either the prophecies were fulfilled or they were not and are still open, or they were altogether wrong.

This is where the Bible is unique. It is, in essence, a book of prophecies of history yet-to-come, and then the historical unfolding of some of the prophesied events was recorded as the actual history occurred. This is continuous throughout the Bible and includes the events in the New Testament. There are also prophecies in the New Testament that have been made but are not yet fulfilled to this day.

This is all very important to understand, and for us to mentally separate. As mentioned in an earlier chapter, some prophecies were clearly stated in the Old Testament and then were validated as having been written before the assembly and translation of the Greek Septuagint, which occurred in the third century BC, well **before** The Christ was born. The Greek Septuagint translation was written about and recorded in **non-**Biblical history texts offering us ample evidence that the prophecies were, in fact, stated and written *before* the prophecies were fulfilled in the New Testament.

Regarding the Old Testament Prophecies that were already fulfilled before the Greek Septuagint was assembled; we have the cross-referential mentioning of some of those prophecies in the later text where the fulfillment was recorded. However, some of them were spoken of in the New Testament and at that time the historical knowledge of the order of events was likely far more familiar to the people who spoke of such events than we are today. When the Christ spoke of the Prophets, he did not do so with any reservations, he spoke with authority regarding them. Since we know through historical testimony that most New Testament events occurred as foretold in the prophecies of the Old Testament, we must take this into consideration when we evaluate the Bible's validity.

There are other ways to validate the prophecies in the Old Testament, and it is with a combination of validation methods that we can be reasonably certain that the prophecies and the subsequent fulfillment of those prophecies actually occurred.

In addition to the past prophecies and the subsequent fulfillment of them, we also have the remaining unfulfilled prophecies. Some people believe that some of the prophecies were to occur a considerable amount of time after the Resurrection of The Christ, but have already occurred relative to our modern day. Many others do not accept that some of those supposed post-Christ fulfillments have occurred. If we must grasp at straws and invent connections in order to force things to match, or if we must ignore portions of the prophecy in order for other more prominent parts of the prophecy to be considered "fulfilled", then we are probably fooling ourselves.

Past prophecies *were not* **kind of** fulfilled, they were completely fulfilled to a fairly refined point of detail. The prophecies yet-to-come are those that are going to be evident to people alive at the time of fulfillment *if* they should happen to occur and those prophecies be *clearly* fulfilled. Prophecies were stated and were written and were witnessed to have been written as a means of repeated attempt to awaken a slumbering people.

And many of those of us alive today can be considered to be a part of those "slumbering people". The prophecies were retained and shared for thousands of years as a cautionary notice to us and as an additional means of evidence that the Bible is valid and that the originator of the Bible does exist.

History

If we ignore the prophecies and consider only the historical events without the foretelling of those events, we still have a retention of Biblical documentation that is backed up by many other valid historical documents, and refuted by only a few people who are of questionable credibility.

When we hear of histories of recorded human events that are claimed to have been written tens of thousands of years ago, we must be cautious in our evaluation of those non-Biblical timelines. I do not suggest that we ignore them altogether; however, there are none that rival the Bible in quantity or accuracy. Most, if not all of these non-Biblical timelines are either modern interpretation of the artifacts, or are utter blind and inventive guesses that some random archeologist suggested a handful of decades ago. None of these timelines involving tens of thousands of years of human history have written documentation describing the details of the events or fully documented timelines.

Invented or interpreted timelines almost all share one key property, which is that they often exceed the timeline of Biblical events by tens of thousands of years. The Bible history and other histories that are clearly written and recorded, shout of consistency and accuracy regarding the Biblical timelines.

Many "Historians" will take a non-Biblical timeline of history that has events similar to the Biblical events, but the timeline is said to be different from the Bible's timeline, thus the supposed "fables" of Bible have nothing to do with the "factual" non-Biblical history–in their minds. Some historians will further go on to claim that the Bible is a series of tales that copied the events of the non-Biblical history. This is, perhaps, ignorance of the highest degree, because when you allow for a "Historian's" poor but rigid timeline to be adjusted to mesh with the Bible's actual written and recorded timeline, then the events typically line up very well and you get a much more robust and clearer view of actual history.

The history written into the Scriptures is vast and robust, yet quite brief when you consider how many events occur in any one person's day-to-day life. The history in the Scriptures, or Biblical writings, was done as a means of evidence of both prophecy and history, and as a message to future people.

Proverbs, Psalms, Songs, and Parables

The other key element of the Scriptures are lessons, or *proverbs*, *psalms*, *songs*, and *parables*. These pieces of scripture are meant to be used as lessons and memorials for subsequent readers or hearers of them to learn from. When someone lives life and has many experiences, especially if they consider God as a part of their life, they typically are able to impart wisdom to others as a guide. This type of wisdom has been written into the proverbs and psalms, etc. as things for people to watch out for in order to avoid making the same mistakes that the author experienced or witnessed.

Psalms and *Songs* were typically scribed as a means of collectively remembering and passing down major details of events that were history-making and usually victorious, often as a means of serving, thanking, and praising God.

Parables were recorded in writing by those who heard Christ tell those parables. The parables are intended to be verbal tools that would help people unfamiliar with a particular concept to better understand that concept through the analogy in the parable *if* their eyes were open and willing. The parables are typically explained immediately after being told and the analogical connections were made so that the point could then become clear to any hearer whose eyes and mind are open and receptive.

Christ mentioned the Scriptures, but when Christ spoke of the "Scripture" he obviously was **not** referring to any of the New Testament. So, the "Scriptures" of today need to be categorized into the parts discussed in the following chapter.

Chapter 18

What is Your Desire?

If you desire to truly understand the Bible, then being able to mentally group or categorize subjects or concepts is critical. If you are unable to do so, then the Bible will generally be a bit foggy to you, making it difficult to achieve your desire to have any definitive understanding of its content. The areas of mental separation of the major parts or types of modern-Scripture are the *Old Testament*, the *Gospels*, the *Epistles*, and finally, *Revelation*.

Understanding the existence of these Scripture groups can clear the way for us to better understand the Epistles. These groups are divided into the *era written* coupled with the *purpose written*. The Old Testament era was written and assembled well before the birth of Jesus The Christ. The Gospels era were written by those contemporary to the events of the four Gospels (Matthew, Mark, Luke, and John). Acts and the Epistles era were written after the Crucifixion and Resurrection and are about events that occurred after the Resurrection and are an effort to tell about or clarify the events that transpired in the Gospels.

And finally, the book of Revelation, which is believed to have been written after the Gospel events had occurred, has many prophecies that were to occur at much later dates.

Epistles Era

The epistles, as mentioned in a previous chapter, are letters. These letters or epistles were written to various individuals or to various peoples by some of Christ's apostles or later followers (James, Peter, John, Jude and Saul-Paul). When looking into the epistles, you will find no shortage of opinion by "scholars" as to the authenticity of authorship, validity, and age of those epistles. The epistles cover a span of roughly sixty years following the Resurrection of Christ, which are the years involved in the initial increase of "Christianity".

The epistles differ from the rest of the Bible in that they tell about the fulfillment of the promise of Salvation, where the rest of the Bible is a written account of the events that comprised Salvation from beginning to end. The Epistles also differ in that they are third-hand information, where the Old Testament is not.

The Old Testament is not someone telling what someone else said. Most of the Old Testament is firsthand or secondhand recording of events. The prophets' of the Old Testament, or someone who penned those books for them, wrote down the prophets' visions or visitations. The historical events of the Old Testament were recorded by the people in charge at the time that those events occurred, or they were recorded by a person in charge of recording such events.

Some of the four Gospels in the New Testament are believed to have been written by firsthand eye-witnesses of the events described in the Gospels. And the epistles tell of those events and of Salvation. The events in the Gospels are events that are historical events that include the words and actions of Jesus The Christ, and in that, they are similar to the Old Testament, but have the addition of being the fulfillment of some of the Old Testament prophecies.

The epistles attempt to interpret and explain some of Jesus The Christ's words. The content of the epistles is much like preachers' sermons of today, but chronologically much closer to the Gospel era. The Saul-Paul epistles are *not* firsthand testimony of Gospel events, but include a claimed visitation to Saul-Paul that caused him to change his ways. Saul-Paul was a Pharisee who was persecuting new Christians as well as those who were teaching other new Christians about The Christ. Before Saul-Paul's claimed vision, his name was "Saul". But after his claimed vision, he was called "Paul". You can sense his Pharisee roots in his attitude and in his often-difficult wording that is typically distorted by most modern preachers.

Many of us choose Saul-Paul's words over Christ's words, which provided that they are in full agreement would not be a problem. However, there are many who pervert Saul-Paul's words to fit their own desired interpretation and then they altogether disregard Christ's words when there is a conflict in interpretation. Saul-Paul also negates rules and then creates new rules that are nowhere to be found in the Bible other than in *his* own writing. This is very problematic and is prominent in Saul-Paul's epistles; yet, much of what he says is accurate.

The order of Authority is: God's words first, then the Prophets ' words, and then Christ's words. Christ's words are more important than the Prophets' words, but without the prophecies we would likely not know or understand that Christ ever existed. In our minds, Jesus would be considered just another prisoner executed by the Romans. The last and least important level of authority is the epistles and the least of those are Saul-Paul's epistles even though they are the dominant portion of those writings and more loved by many preachers than are the words of all of the rest of the Bible.

It is important to understand that the key purpose of the Bible is the message of Salvation. When the Apostles went abroad to share this "Good News" message with people, the New Testament did not yet exist–it was being lived and written *at that time*, and was *not* a part of "Scripture". The Apostles were, by today's standards, preachers. They were telling of, or clarifying, Christ and Salvation and how that all connected to the *Old Testament*, or at that time, "the Scriptures". This makes the epistles very different than the rest of the Bible, and we must use caution when attempting to understand the epistles. Always look at God's words and God's words through the Prophets and God's words through The Christ first and use *them* as your foundation for understanding the Bible *before* using the epistles to build your foundation. The epistles were never meant to be a written foundation, rather they were telling about the foundation.

If our interpretation of the epistles does not agree with the rest of the Bible, especially the Saul-Paul epistles, then either we are interpreting them wrong, or there are translation errors within them, or those who wrote epistles were wrong in some of what they wrote. If you cannot accept this simple truth, then you can be pretty certain that you *will* be deceived about God's words at some point in the future if you are not already at this time.

Use caution when reading the epistles. Saul-Paul's writings in particular are frequently used in circular reasoning and cause many to turn from God due to the anomalies in this particular circular reasoning that we all too often use. I have found no other part of the Bible where circular reasoning is used in such an abusive manner as it is with Saul-Paul's epistles. But we cannot see this when we place Saul-Paul ahead of The Christ and The Christ's words. Always look at *all* of **God's Words first**, and make sure that you *never* use circular reasoning when analyzing anything in the Bible.

Acts

The book of Acts stands apart from the epistles because it is not a simple letter of correction to anyone. Rather, it is partly a continuation of the documentation laid out in the four Gospels, or more to the point, it is a continuation of Luke's Gospel. The history recorded in Acts assists in putting some of the other epistles into geographic context as well as epistle content context.

If you read through the book of Acts and the other epistles you should see Saul-Paul's epistles stand out in a peculiar way that makes them suspect of inaccuracy or mistranslation or misinterpretation. The authority given to the twelve apostles was done in the Gospels. And Saul-Paul, while claiming to be an "apostle", was not actually one of them and must not be considered so. So, Saul-Paul's writings stand out in that way, and when you are aware you will see this in Acts and in the other epistles. Read the epistles carefully and read Acts and the Gospels carefully making sure to first consider God's Words, God's Words through the Prophets, and God's Words through The Christ *before* you consider any of the epistles.

If your desire is to truly understand the Bible, then making a mental separation between Saul-Paul's writings versus the rest of the entire Bible is critical to your ability to understand the entire Bible. Saul-Paul and his epistles are a point of division between the various religions and also between God and religion *and* between God and the Church. Gather your thoughts and your logic if you truly desire to harvest the unending Truth offered in the Bible.

Those who follow Saul-Paul over The Christ are many, and they can and often will rationalize any point you can imagine ranging from abortion to lifestyle choices to infidelity. The divisions that have been allowed and have been caused as a result of the Saul-Paul epistles are many as is seen in the many factions of the "Christian" faiths that arose during and after the

Reformation of the 1500s. Some of this is discussed in the book *Understanding The Church.*

Chapter 19

Retaining What You Read

I find that people learn in one of two ways. Some people will read and remember but they need to remember each detail in the instructions in order to carry out a task. But there is a lesser quantity of others who will grasp an overall-concept and therefore have a clearer view of the task at hand, thus allowing them to proceed with confidence and an ability to easily complete that task as well as many other similar tasks. Those who seek a birds-eye view of any task or subject are generally not as burdened with details, yet they can still see those details and how they relate to the overall view when they find or hear of the details.

Those who remember every detail and see only the details-view have a sort of can't-see-thee-forest-through-the-trees problem as we recklessly follow preachers who tell us *how it is* rather than them telling us to read and grasp the bigger picture for ourselves.

There would not be a problem with those who see only the details but fail on the bigger picture if we did not create doctrine of our own. But since many have created their own doctrine, we have over the years prompted evermore divisions of religion and of people, and we have turned many people from God and from Salvation by doing so.

How You Remember

The world needs both *detail* people and *overall-view* people. Those of us who have a gift or affinity for detail can be a danger to ourselves because we cannot see past our current point of reference or interest. This blocks us from realizing that other new critical information exists that connects to our current understanding. And then, if and when we read new information, we get so stuck in our new point of interest to where we lose sight of our first point of reference. This blocks us from being able to see the connections between our old point *A* and our new point *B*. This also causes us to make improper connections between other points that should *not* be connected at all. When we are able to see a clearer overall view, we then find other points in the Bible's text that reveal that our improper connections are in fact improper.

Those who view the bigger picture with an overall-view methodology have a much better handle on the overall contents of the Bible, but we often lack the ability to concisely state details of something we might be familiar with, and thus cannot articulate it with much evidentiary detail without reviewing the information.

Neither of these two methods of remembering the text of the Bible are wrong, but because those who focus on detail are often those who invent new theories, it is problematic. However, when both types of memories come together and can clearly prove their cases to one another, it expands understanding for people who have either memory type. Having an overall-view is better and safer than a detailed-view, but if your overall-view lacks detail then you will be incapable of articulating a sound presentation of your perspective to a willing ear, and thus you might unintentionally deceive them, or accidentally direct them to a person who articulates details dangerously. Be aware that these two types of memory exist and understand them and which type matches your memory habits. It is a good thing to be aware of about yourself.

Store Up Information

Try to first concern yourself with *God's Words, and then God's Words through the Prophets, and finally God's Words through The Christ,* and then try to get a good overall view of the Bible through those words. It is then that the history of the Bible will begin to have substantial relevance in your mind. Otherwise it all becomes a bunch of disconnected trivia that we attempt to force connections between according to the guidance of the preachers' and teachers' opinions that we hear.

We are all entitled to our own opinions, and when we drop the legalistic nonsense, it is far easier for everyone to see the bigger picture without getting mired down in false details of the opinions of the minions who are the false preachers. When we do this it is easier for all to agree on the meaning, because we are then listening to God rather than to man.

When we hear of "false preachers", we tend to think of deliberate deception, which does occur. But a "false preacher," or false teacher, is simply someone who is teaching false doctrine. That is to say, doctrine that is not accurate, even if it is being done with the purest of intentions.

The Law says "Thou shalt not steal", but if a preacher can convince you that it is okay to steal, then, is it really okay to steal because a preacher permitted it? I realize that this is a simplified extreme example, but it does clearly illustrate that what we believe or are told is *not* necessarily what is true. Use caution in what information you store up because it *will* affect all of your subsequent decisions and actions and paths you choose to follow and study. It will also affect which verses and books in the Bible you choose to dwell on. It is the pieces of information you choose to store up that determines if *you* will follow *God's Words* or man's words. We can't take pieces of the Bible and piece them together in an ad-hoc manner and then expect to come to proper conclusions, a technique that many of us have a tendency to do. If our conclusions don't match the overall messages in the Bible, then we are certain to have erred in our conclusions.

Chapter 20

Representatives of God

What is a "Representative" of God? We are *all* representatives of God. Some of us are more substantially representatives, such as the ultimate representative, The Christ, followed by the Prophets. Whether we are good or evil, all of us are still ultimately "representatives of God". And since the Bible clearly indicates God's distaste for evil, we can then understand why representatives who practice evil are rejected, or at least strongly rebuked by God.

The Face Of God

Humans *are* the face of God. Having been created in God's image, we represent God. So it stands to reason that if this God does in fact exist, as the Bible indicates, then our defiance of the natural laws embodied in the Ten Commandments would be quite offensive to the God who set them in place in our hearts and minds to begin with.

When you review all of the chapters in this book and force yourself to reason through the points of logic mentioned within, while keeping in mind the mental separations that clear our view of the Bible, you should be able to ascertain easily, on your own, the validity of the Bible. This will assist in eliminating any suggestion that the Bible is "just a bunch of stories that someone made up" or that "the Bible is a book of mere fables and myths".

Even if you are a self-proclaimed atheist, you are still representing God, maybe poorly so, but a representative nonetheless. However, it is important to note that there are some atheists who are better representatives than are many "Christians". "But, how can this be possible?" you might ask.

If someone is an atheist and is honest when discussing the Biblical text and is sharing their thoughts and those thoughts are accurate to the Bible, and if they are not trying to deceive people or detour them from God; then while you might consider them foolish, they are at least not liars and are accurate and honest. If their information is accurate and true, then God will not count that against them, though their *denial* of God will be counted against them.

Then on the Christian's side, we see few, but far too many, people fouling the meaning of many statements in the Bible, thus creating false doctrine, and then teaching that false doctrine to others. They do this while clearly indicating that they believe in God and that the Jesus The Christ is the Savior. But their false doctrine will be held against them, and the harm that they did to others through their inaccuracies will also be held against them— so indicates the Bible. This false doctrine has created many atheists and often the atheists mistakenly believe this false doctrine is what the Bible actually says and thus they have turned from God due to lies.

You are a representative of God, and only *you* can choose if you are going to be a good representative or not a good representative. Our choice of being an atheist or a Christian has the same level of importance as the accuracy of what we believe and of what we share and teach to others. Seek to be a good representative by being accurate, because when you are accurate you are far more likely to recognize Truth when you cross its path. Truth is not exclusive to Christians, it is exclusive to all those who seek and pursue it when they truly find it. But it is important to understand that someone can be an atheist and be very accurate about the Bible text, but still not believe in God or, more importantly, in Salvation, and that might prove to be a problem for them at some point in their future.

Men, Women, and Family

The relationship between Man and Woman is clearly analogical of the relationship between humans and God. Marriage represents our connection to God. However, since there are so many failed marriages, the Husband and Wife analogy unfairly harms our understanding and view of humanity's **intended** relationship to God. This is discussed more in the book *Red Hot Marriage*.

This analogy holds true whether the marriages are failed or joyous. This is because failed relationships do exist in our marriages and also between humans and God. If we fail to see God's desire for a good relationship between us and God then we are also likely to have a poor relationship with our spouse and a poor relationship with God.

When trying to figure out certain things regarding the Bible, look at the family unit and think about *the way things **should** be* between family members, rather than the way things all too often are. It is very likely that you understand what is meant in saying "*the way things **should** be*". Understanding what is meant by "*the way things **should** be*" clearly indicates that we **all** understand. Use that thought to help yourself grasp what God truly desires of us humans. If we have an evil heart, it is possible that we have made ourselves incapable of seeing the obvious connection between our marriages and God's desire for us. But even if our heart is *not* evil, we can still damage our relationship between God and ourselves by following the wrong shepherds.

The husband and wife analogy can reveal a great deal of Biblical text that is hidden in plain sight due to the veil of fog that clouds our minds. Utilizing the husband and wife analogy and *properly* applying it and/or recognizing that it is used in Biblical text, will help to pull the veil back to reveal to you much previously unrealized text.

Comparison

The Bible is filled with analogies and examples in the form of parables and proverbs, but there are also analogies in many prophecies. These comparisons help us to understand a broader concept that we would otherwise not be able to comprehend or notice. The analogies are a type of mental separation, and it is mental separation that allows us to compare one thing to another.

When we lack the ability to mentally separate issues, we are incapable of comparing the topics that require mental separation to understand them. For instance, accepting Saul-Paul as equal to the other apostles obscures our view of the text he wrote, and thus, we see him and his words as having the same authority as the other Apostles, or even the same authority as God's Words, or God's Words through the Prophets, or God's Words through Jesus The Christ. When we do this, it then allows us to use Saul-Paul's words **in place of** *God's Words through Christ*. There is a *difference* in those two sets of words, that is to say Saul-Paul's words versus God's words, and that difference is there to see for those who choose to find it.

Saul-Paul's words say one thing and God's Words say another. Whose are the proper words, Saul-Paul's or God's? Peter, who The Christ himself declared the stone on which the Church would be built, did specifically comment on Saul-Paul's writings. From the Douay Rheims Bible II Peter 3:15-18 "15 And account the longsuffering of our Lord, salvation; as also our most dear brother Paul, according to the wisdom given him, hath written to you: 16 As also in all his epistles, speaking in them of these things; in which are certain things hard to be understood, which the unlearned and unstable wrest, as they do also the other scriptures, to their own destruction. 17 You therefore, brethren, knowing these things before, take heed, lest being led aside by the error of the unwise, you fall from your own steadfastness. 18 But grow in grace, and in the knowledge of our Lord and Savior Jesus Christ. To Him be glory both now and unto the day of eternity. Amen."

Use comparison properly and make sure **God's Words** are *your* authority. You will find a great deal of understanding in them as you read and study the Bible. You will also notice that God's Words through The Christ coincide with God's Words in the Old Testament, but only when using Truth to interpret the text.

Chapter 21

Lost Books and Other Differences

Some of the topics in this book, *Understanding The Bible*, are difficult to cut short because the Bible and these topics are all so very intertwined in such a way that it is difficult to discuss any of it without diving into the details of other aspects of the Bible when discussing one specific aspect. You might have noticed, there is a central theme in this book having to do with our ability to define clear mental distinctions between things that trip us up as we venture into reading and/or studying the Bible. I would prefer to not even share these things and instead let everyone discover these points for themselves because there is so much value in discovering things by ourselves. However, since many of these mental separations are not *ever* realized by most people, including many so-called scholars, it causes us to needlessly turn from the Bible and from God, and this book is here to help stop that error.

When you understand the assembly of the Bible and the needed mental separations regarding it, you can categorize the aspects of the Bible in to historical, prophetic, educational, etc. as well as into chronological groups of pre-Christ, during-Christ, and post-Christ eras.

Lost Books

As you dive into reading the Bible or studying it you are bound to come across some of the "Lost books of the Bible" that were spoken of in a previous chapter and referred to as pseudepigrapha. There are many such writings that can add to our understanding of the Bible, but many of those writings can also harm our understanding of the Bible when we lack understanding. There are writings from each era of the Bible, pre-Christ, during-Christ, and post-Christ. Most of the writings listed in this book are very complimentary to the Biblical information, but there are other writings that are suspect of being fabricated and are fraudulent, but they are old.

In this we judge ourselves worthy, or not worthy, by what from these writing we choose to believe. Some of these writings are believed to have been written during the Acts-Epistles era and may be referred to in the epistles where we are warned against false teachings. Here is a recap of the list of a *sampling* of the more prominent writings of antiquity that are mostly complimentary to the Old Testament of the Bible:

1. Apocalypse of Abraham
2. Books of Adam and Eve
3. Apocalypse of Adam
4. Syriac, Apocalypse of Baruch
5. Biblical Antiquities
6. Book of Enoch
7. Book of the Secrets of Enoch
8. Fourth Book of Ezra (2 Esdras)
9. Books of Giants
10. Book of Jubilees
11. Lives of the Prophets
12. Fourth Book of Maccabees

13. Testament of Moses
14. Sibylline Oracles
15. Testament of Solomon
16. Testaments of the Twelve Patriarchs

And from the New Testament of the Bible:
17. The Gospel of Thomas
18. The Gospel of Peter
19. The Gospel of Mary
20. The Epistle of Barnabas

For this subject we have to go back to the assembly and translation of the Greek Septuagint and to the assembly and translation of the Latin Vulgate. There are certain books in the Old Testament that are in all Bibles and they are your foundational books. All other writings should coincide with those particular books–the New Testament Gospels refer to these Old Testament books. And then Acts and the Epistles generally refer to the Gospels or the events within them. Jesus the Christ did have his own teachings, but they were largely based on Old Testament documents. Jesus also quoted the Old Testament Scriptures and regarded them highly.

The key Bible books of the Old Testament should be our foundation together with the Gospels regarding Biblical study. Acts and the Epistles and some of the Pseudepigrapha are from the era of both the Old and New Testaments and can all offer a great deal of insight on many of the peculiar statements made in the Bible. There are many statements in the Bible that appear arbitrary and seem to be very odd and disconnected statements, but some of those odd statements are detailed and clarified in some of the pseudepigraphal writings. Because there are so many of those writings, we must use care and logic in reviewing and analyzing them. Just as it is today, back then there were those who didn't believe Salvation or in God at that time and some of them recorded their thoughts in writing (those writings are not listed in this book). There were also those who innocently had incorrect information and recorded their thoughts. So, how do we tell what is true amongst these extra books?

Telling what is "true" is not so much the point, as is determining what is *accurate* to the overall picture. The issue of finding what is "true" comes down to a personal point of belief based upon *accurate* evidence. There is little other choice than for us to approach these writings like a jury, where you gather the information and discuss it to try to fit the pieces together to see which pieces fit and agree with the larger collection of writings, versus those that clearly do not agree. However, when doing so, we must rid ourselves of our biases. It's okay to have a starting opinion, but a *bias* will cause you to judge in a biased manner and often wrongly so.

Starting opinion or starting thoughts, if *not* biased, will quickly change when we see what is true, but a biased opinion will typically not change even when truth is clearly made evident. Biased opinions are based on *emotion* rather than on the *true facts*, and those biases lead to a rift between people, causing sides to be taken. The sometimes-annoying push-back, regardless of our position, can be used for good, because it challenges us to find alternate verification of our thoughts *if* such verification can be found. We need to keep calm and be rational when discussing conflicting thoughts from other people, and we must be open to hearing other people's opinions and their analysis of our own thoughts so that we can consider whether or not our own thoughts are valid.

Problems with Us-Against-Them

Our biases cause us a great deal of trouble when analyzing these ancient writings. If you get deep into studying ancient histories, you will quickly find opposing sides as to the validity of the ancient documents—and there are more than a few sides in these debates. This typically causes tension and finger pointing at error in opinion. However, if you can free yourself of other people's biases and free yourself from your own biases, you can learn a great deal from the various conflicting opinions, provided that you are able to filter out *biased opinion* from the *actual facts* in any discussion. Our ability to mentally separate *fact* from *bias* is critical in honest analysis, and it is rare in any of us. Stay clear of the us-against-them mentality so that you can discover the actual facts and hear other people's information and analyze it and then judge it fairly.

The Real Ten Commandments

What do you mean the "Real" Ten Commandments? Do you mean to tell me that there are more "Ten Commandments" sets than the set we think exists? Yes and no. The Ten Commandments are first given in Exodus 20:2-17 and then are reiterated in Deuteronomy 5:6-21. Here are both for your evaluation.

Douay Rheims Exodus 20:1-17

1 And the Lord spoke all these words: 2 I am the Lord thy God, who brought thee out of the land of Egypt, out of the house of bondage. 3 Thou shalt not have strange gods before me. 4 Thou shalt not make to thyself a graven thing, nor the likeness of anything that is in heaven above, or in the earth beneath, nor of those things that are in the waters under the earth. 5 Thou shalt not adore them, nor serve them: I am the Lord thy God, mighty, jealous, visiting the iniquity of the fathers upon the children, unto the third and fourth generation of them that hate me:

6 And shewing mercy unto thousands to them that love me, and keep my commandments. 7 Thou shalt not take the name of the Lord thy God in vain: for the Lord will not hold him guiltless that shall take the name of the Lord his God in vain. 8 Remember that thou keep holy the sabbath day. 9 Six days shalt thou labor, and shalt do all thy works. 10 But on the seventh day is the sabbath of the Lord thy God: thou shalt do no work on it, thou nor thy son, nor thy daughter, nor thy manservant, nor thy maidservant, nor thy beast, nor the stranger that is within thy gates.

11 For in six days the Lord made heaven and earth, and the sea, and all things that are in them, and rested on the seventh day: therefore, the Lord blessed the seventh day, and sanctified it. 12 Honor thy father and thy mother,

that thou mayest be long-lived upon the land which the Lord thy God will give thee. 13 Thou shalt not kill. 14 Thou shalt not commit adultery. 15 Thou shalt not steal.

16 Thou shalt not bear false witness against thy neighbor. 17 Thou shalt not covet thy neighbor's house: neither shalt thou desire his wife, nor his servant, nor his handmaid, nor his ox, nor his ass, nor any thing that is his

The Ten Commandments in Douay Rheims Deuteronomy 5:5-21

5 I was the mediator and stood between the Lord and you at that time, to shew you his words, for you feared the fire, and went not up into the mountain, and he said:

6 I am the Lord thy God, who brought thee out of the land of Egypt, out of the house of bondage. 7 Thou shalt not have strange gods in my sight. 8 Thou shalt not make to thyself a graven thing, nor the likeness of any things, that are in heaven above, or that are in the earth beneath, or that abide in the waters under the earth. 9 Thou shalt not adore them, and thou shalt not serve them. For I am the Lord thy God, a jealous God, visiting the iniquity of the fathers upon their children unto the third and fourth generation, to them that hate me, 10 And shewing mercy unto many thousands, to them that love me, and keep my commandments.

11 Thou shalt not take the name of the Lord thy God in vain: for he shall not be unpunished that taketh his name upon a vain thing. 12 Observe the day of the sabbath, to sanctify it, as the Lord thy God hath commanded thee. 13 Six days shalt thou labor, and shalt do all thy works. 14 The seventh is the day of the sabbath, that is, the rest of the Lord thy God. Thou shalt not do any work therein, thou nor thy son nor thy daughter, nor thy manservant nor thy maidservant, nor thy ox, nor thy ass, nor any of thy beasts, nor the stranger that is within thy gates: that thy manservant and thy maidservant may rest, even as thyself. 15 Remember that thou also didst serve in Egypt, and the Lord thy God brought thee out from thence with a strong hand, and a stretched-out arm. Therefore, hath he commanded thee that thou should observe the sabbath day.

16 Honor thy father and mother, as the Lord thy God hath commanded thee, that thou mayst live a long time, and it may be well with thee in the land, which the Lord thy God will give thee. 17 Thou shalt not kill. 18 Neither shalt thou commit adultery. 19 And thou shalt not steal. 20 Neither shalt thou bear false witness against thy neighbor.

21 Thou shalt not covet thy neighbor's wife: nor his house, nor his field, nor his manservant, nor his maidservant, nor his ox, nor his ass, nor any thing that is his.

You'll notice that these two texts, Exodus 20:2-17 Deuteronomy 5:6-21, are not perfectly identical in the way that they are phrased. They were likely not stated identically word-for-word originally, but had identical intent. Through the various Bible translations, the two versions can become worded differently even more so. Some Ten Commandments lists will be taken from Exodus 20:2-17, where others will be taken from Deuteronomy 5:6-21. Now add to this the simplification of the Commandments for display purposes and you end up with some noticeable differences between the various Ten Commandments versions that we might come across today.

They are generally consistent in meaning, but there are those Bible versions that state the commandments in such a way that it can cause a difference in the one-through-ten list. This is a point that is often brought up by opponents of the Bible in effort to discredit the Bible. But do not let this dissuade you from reading the Bible. Instead it should make us curious as to why there would be any difference at all in any Ten Commandments lists presented by any church, religion, group, or the Bible itself.

However, there is another often overlooked version of commandments that is not as clearly laid out as the other two lists are. This list of commands is interspersed with other instruction as Moses prepared two stone tablets to replace the Ten Commandments tablets that Moses demolished:

Douay Rheims Exodus 34:1-29

"1 And after this he said: Hew thee two tables of stone like unto the former, and I will write upon them the words which were in the tables, which thou brokest. 2 Be ready in the morning, that thou mayst forthwith go up into mount Sinai, and thou shalt stand with me upon the top of the mount. 3 Let no man go up with thee: and let not any man be seen throughout all the mount: neither let the oxen nor the sheep feed over against it. 4 Then he cut out two tables of stone, such as had been before: and rising very early he went up into the mount Sinai, as the Lord had commanded him, carrying with him the tables. 5 And when the Lord was come down in a cloud, Moses stood with him, calling upon the name of the Lord.

6 And when he passed before him, he said: O the Lord, the Lord God, merciful and gracious, patient and of much compassion, and true, 7 Who keepest mercy unto thousands: who takest away iniquity, and wickedness, and sin, and no man of himself is innocent before thee. Who renderest the iniquity of the fathers to the children, and to the grandchildren, unto the third and fourth generation. 8 And Moses making haste, bowed down prostrate unto the earth, and adoring, 9 Said: If I have found grace in thy sight: O Lord, I beseech thee, that thou wilt go with us, (for it is a stiffnecked people,) and take away our iniquities and sin, and possess us. 10 The Lord answered: I will make a covenant in the sight of all. I will do signs such as were never seen upon the earth, nor in any nation: that this people, in the midst of whom thou art, may see the terrible work of the Lord which I will do.

11 Observe all things which this day I command thee: I myself will drive out before thy face the Amorrhite, and the Chanaanite, and the Hethite, and the Pherezite, and the Hevite, and the Jebusite. 12 Beware thou never join in friendship with the inhabitants of that land, which may be thy ruin: 13 But destroy their altars, break their statues, and cut down their groves: 14 Adore not any strange god. The Lord his name is Jealous, he is a jealous God. 15 Make no covenant with the men of those countries lest, when they have committed fornication with their gods, and have adored their idols, some one call thee to eat of the things sacrificed.

16 Neither shalt thou take of their daughters a wife for thy son, lest after they themselves have committed fornication, they make thy sons also to commit fornication with their gods. 17 Thou shalt not make to thyself any molten gods. 18 Thou shalt keep the feast of the unleavened bread. Seven days shalt thou eat unleavened bread, as I commanded thee in the time of the month of the new corn: for in the month of the springtime thou camest out from Egypt. 19 All of the male kind, that openeth the womb, shall be mine. Of all beasts, both of oxen and of sheep, it shall be mine. 20 The firstling of an ass thou shalt redeem with a sheep: but if thou wilt not give a price for it, it shall be slain. The firstborn of thy sons thou shalt redeem: neither shalt thou appear before me empty.

21 Six days shalt thou work, the seventh day thou shalt cease to plough, and to reap. 22 Thou shalt keep the feast of weeks with the first fruits of the corn of thy wheat harvest, and the feast when the time of the year returned that all things are laid in. 23 Three times in a year all thy males shall appear in the sight of the Almighty Lord the God of Israel. 24 For when I shall have taken away the nations from thy face, and shall have enlarged thy borders, no man shall lie in wait against thy land when thou shalt go up, and appear in the

sight of the Lord thy God thrice in a year. 25 Thou shalt not offer the blood of my sacrifice upon leaven: neither shall there remain in the morning anything of the victim of the solemnity of the Lord.

26 The first of the fruits of thy ground thou shalt offer in the house of the Lord thy God. Thou shalt not boil a kid in the milk of his dam. 27 And the Lord said to Moses: Write these words by which I have made a covenant both with thee and with Israel. 28 And he was there with the Lord forty days and forty nights: he neither ate bread nor drank water, and he wrote upon the tables the ten words of the covenant. 29 And when Moses came down from the mount Sinai, he held the two tables of the testimony,"

Depending upon which text is used, the commandments can appear very different. However, the Exodus 34:1-29 text is *not* the Ten Commandments, nor is it claimed to be so in the text itself, even though some of the Ten Commandment are incorporated in this text. Exodus 34:1 indicates "And after this he said: Hew thee two tables of stone like unto the former, and *I* will write upon them the words which were in the tables, which thou brokest". And then Exodus 34:27 says "And the Lord said to Moses: Write these words by which I have made a covenant both with thee and with Israel." Some people take this to be an instruction for Moses to write down those words on the tablets of stone. But that is *not* what the text says.

While an honest reading of the text indicates that Moses was to carve two tablets and then the Lord said "*I* will write upon them the words which were in the tables, which thou brokest.", it does not say that *Moses* would write anything on the tablets. Moses was to write down what God was saying while the Lord was making a duplicate of the original Ten Commandments that Moses smashed during his fit of anger against the Israelites for transgressing against God after God had saved them from Egyptian slavery and they walked through the divided sea and then watched the released sea defeat pharaoh's army, etc. The Exodus 34:1-29 text is both an additional rebuke and additional instructions along with prophecy to help the Israelites clarify a few points of understanding regarding their position relative to God's position. It is not a listing of the Ten Commandments like Exodus 20:2-17 and Deuteronomy 5:6-21 are, nor was it ever meant to be. Do not be deceived by those who claim the Ten Commandments are different in various parts of the Bible.

There are many who are either deliberately trying to deceive others by misapplying these texts, or are doing it out of utter blindness, or ignorance, and possibly laziness in that we fail to work to verify claims that do not seem quite right.

Bible reading and Bible study have never been easier, or more dangerous, than in our technological era were every opinion is immediately available and posted and text messaged to the world. Use caution in who you follow. If you recall, there is one "Good Shepherd", but we often fail to follow that one Good Shepherd and instead we follow Saul-Paul or other questionable shepherds through their books and writings that we find using technology. There is no end to the quantity of opinions on these matters. Too often, we are followers rather than researchers. Followers often get off track because "there are many who will come in my name" as Jesus The Christ said in Matthew 24 warning us of frauds who will try to cleverly deceive us and claim to be leading us to Christ, but they do not do so. Choose to study while being ever mindful of Truth, rather than blindly following others.

Other Information

There is more information to be discovered, but there is a great wealth of existing information already available today to those of us who choose to look for it. There are countless archeological finds of artifacts, places, and writings, most of which reinforces the Bible's text to a point of certainty. But the timelines that are often arbitrarily attached to these archeological finds usually do not match with the Bible's written historical timeline, yet everything else about them does match. When this is the case, then who do we believe? Do we believe the person who invents a timeline based upon their own best guess? Or do we believe the timelines that are actually laid down written within ancient texts of the Bible, and then use them to connect the other archeological finds to Biblical timelines? The answer here is obvious to any honest researcher.

Chapter 22

Time for Choices

We discussed a bit about miracles in an earlier chapter and the fact that a "miracle" is something that does not ordinarily occur but will put us in a state of awe. Miracles are miracles because they are miracles. If these so-called "miracles" did not amaze the people at the time that they occurred, then they would likely not have been written down and recorded for future generations to read about. We do similar notation today in the form of news when something out of the ordinary occurs. But the events that we record today are typically bad news and are not really awe inspiring at all. Miracles, on the other hand, are typically good news as well as being events that awed people.

What we choose to decide to believe about miracles is up to each one of us. And it is our analysis of the text of the Bible and supporting texts and evidence that will determine the outcome of our decision regarding the legitimacy of the good and bad miracles documented in the Bible.

Good Miracles

Many of the "good" miracles in the Bible lack concrete evidence. Bringing a dead person back to life is truly amazing, but not much more than written eyewitness testimony is available regarding such events, thus making them difficult to prove today. However, *lack* of evidence can be somewhat convincing evidence of people rising from the dead. The whole point of Salvation was to allow people to be able to return to God, and the Bible tells of such promises and of people rising from the dead and those people eventually being taken up to Heaven. Now, all of that is difficult to prove, however, the absence of graves and bones of the risen people is somewhat indicative of having risen from the dead because the graves are known but empty.

We find abundant evidence of graves and bones of pharaohs and even priests from Jesus The Christ's time. And we find many other prominent graves all with bones still in them, but what we don't find are the graves or bones of the key people of the Bible who were thought to be righteous, such as Adam, Able, Seth, Noah, Abraham, Isaac, Jacob, and Jesus. This absence can be taken as them not having ever existed, but then we have to question the other people mentioned in the Bible whose graves and bones **have been found**. Combining these points illustrates the absence of the righteous and of them possibly having risen from the dead, thus causing their obvious absence in any archeological finds.

Other miracles, such as Jesus Christ having just a small amount of fish and bread to work with and then miraculously feeding five-thousand and then at a later time another four-thousand people, are not likely to ever be proven with specific evidence, especially because the evidence was eaten by the nine-thousand total people in those two cases. For these types of miracles, we have to rely on the actual written testimony.

Another miracle that would only have written eyewitness testimony is Jesus and Peter walking on water. Other than some of Peter's wet clothing that would now be dry, this particular miracle would not have produced any lasting evidence whatsoever. There are other such miracles like healing the blind and making the lame walk etc., but all of these good miracles left behind no concrete evidence to prove to us today that they actually occurred. Written eye witness testimony is all that we have to go on as evidence regarding some of the miracles.

Amongst the Good Miracles is that of the Body and Blood of Christ. This particular issue is a point of contention between some of the various religions, where one religion says that when some receives the communion host/wafer and the wine that they are receiving the actual Body and Blood of Christ, where others say it is only symbolic. This particular issue is not a Biblical issue as one might categorize it. Those who believe that it is the actual Body and Blood of Christ are often mocked as "cannibals" by their atheist peers due to the fact that they would be eating The Christ. But there is another view of this practice and it is that Christ or Christ's Holy Spirit is present in the communion bread and wine, which is an entirely different perspective and very logical. In the Bible The Christ said "This is my Body" when breaking bread with the apostles during his last supper, but what we don't know is if this was intended to be an analogy or if Christ actually meant that the bread he held was his body, which is further discussed in *Understanding The Church*.

If Heaven exists, you will likely find out when you get there. It seems more likely that Christ was trying to establish a long-standing tradition by saying "Do this in remembrance of me" as he took the bread and ate it and drank the wine and then shared with his Apostles. Regardless of whether or not this is a specific "Good Miracle", Christ did very soundly establish a very long-standing tradition of teaching it from one generation to the next for about two-thousand years. And *that* is truly a Good Miracle.

While we can doubt these good miracles, it is difficult to doubt the events surrounding them given the other evidence and written documentation supporting the other non-miracle events that occurred during those times. The validity of the other events does lend to the credibility of the written accounts of these miraculous events, even though it does not prove them to have occurred. Are there other means that can lend some credibility to "good" miracles?

Bad Miracles

Bad miracles are miracles that were used to prove God's superiority over man. Some of us might want to make God out to be some sort of big bully for having done bad miracles, but those miracles were never done without some sort of pre-warning or knowledge of wrongdoing by the recipients of bad type miracles.

Let's consider the miracles that were the many plagues of Egypt. Pharaoh was at first politely asked to let the Israelites go free. In fact, their initial request was to only be able to leave the area to worship their God periodically. But Pharaoh refused to cooperate, and his resistance angered God, which caused the miraculous successive plague events to eventually occur. After continued warnings, and continued stubbornness on Pharaoh's part, the miraculous plagues eventually ended in the death of all of the first-born in Egypt if they failed to mark their door posts and lentils on the night that death came so that death could Passover them. Death would have passed over them if they had followed the instructions. None of these plagues would have left much evidence other than possible residue from blood and frog remains and such that might be found in mass quantity if we were to dig around in that area today.

However, things change a bit once the Israelites leave Egypt. After pharaoh was finally defeated and agreed to let the Israelites go due to all of the miraculous but devastating plagues, he decided to set out after the Israelites in one final attempt to take revenge on the Israelites for the devastation that had come upon Egypt at the hand of God through Moses. After the Israelites departed from Egypt, they were pressed against the sea and cornered with no weapons and no place to go.

As the army of Pharaoh approached the Israelites to slaughter them, the Israelites began to fear and doubt, then God set a pillar of fire between Pharaoh's army and the Israelites in effort to stop Pharaoh and his army from advancing on the Israelites, and also to display's God's power. At this point the Israelites were still trapped and had nowhere to go, so, to show God's might, God had Moses hold up his staff and the sea parted before the people of Israel and they crossed through the sea on dry ground.

As they were completing their passage through the divisions in the sea, the pillar of fire that God had placed before Pharaoh dissipated and Pharaoh's army then descended into the divided sea to pursue the Israelites. As the Israelites completed their crossing, Pharaoh's whole army was completely within the passages between the divided water, and the water was then released and went back to its normal position. Pharaoh's entire army with all of their armor and chariots and weapons and horses were drowned. This would have been a truly horrifying experience for Pharaoh, but to the Israelites it probably brought on a great sense of awe and relief. Is this miracle that is both *bad* and *good* true? Can it be proven? I will let you be the judge of that, but since Pharaoh's *entire* army was drowned in the water, you would think that there would be some remnants of evidence still in existence in that sea to this day.

Other bad miracles are those that destroyed cities, such as with fire and brimstone raining down upon Sodom and Gomorrah. The region where Sodom and Gomorrah were located should have some evidence of the cataclysmic event that destroyed the cities. If we were to find brimstone in that area, then that would be pretty good evidence that some such catastrophe did in fact occur there at some point in time past.

There is evidence out there for us to utilize when validating these miraculous claims, but we won't find what we don't look for. The flood is another miraculous catastrophe that should present some evidence, and depending upon your analysis of geology, the evidence of massive floods is found *everywhere* on Earth. However, this only proves that massive flooding occurred, it does not prove that it occurred simultaneously all over the Earth. Information regarding the flood is further discussed in the book *The Science of God-Volume 5 - The Flood.*

There is evidence out there, but you must eventually make up your own mind as to what is evidence enough for *you* to accept the accounts of any of the miracles as actually having occurred. This is one of those areas that, regardless of what we choose to believe regarding the miracles, it is irrelevant as to whether or not they actually occurred. Imagine for a moment that someone rejects the evidence and the entire premise of miracles. Will their rejection of evidence make the person correct if the miracles actually **did** occur? No, it will not.

We are told by Christ that if we seek, we shall find. I see a whole lot of opining and very little seeking done by most of us, especially regarding finding hard evidence of these catastrophic miracles. I am not saying that people have not found such evidence, I am saying that we are typically too lazy to even bother finding the evidence that others have already found. It is impressive what you can readily find today because of what many people have been doing for centuries in this regard, if only you take the time and make the effort to actually look.

Consider this chapter carefully because it is about the most unusual events. These super miraculous events seem like the most unlikely to ever be proven, especially if they did not occur, yet they might be the most provable parts of the entire Bible. What if evidence has been found, what then do we make of these events? Seek, and you might find that there is evidence to luminate the path **if** you so choose to look for it. Ask and you shall receive!

Chapter 23

Ask and You Shall Receive

I have met very few people who have entered study of the Bible *without* an agenda to prove their own particular point. Of course, there's nothing wrong with entering study with an agenda *if* you are open to other thoughts and evidence that refute your perspective. We all ignore evidence to some extent–all of us!

Evidence has a funny way of appearing when you look for it as is described in the chapter mentioning the-red-car-effect. It is only when we are able to form a concept within our mind that we are able to recognize any evidence for what it is, whether for or against our own belief. If you have children you might recall that you may have told them things scores of times and it did not register with them, but once they had children of their own, all of a sudden they were able to see what you had previously told them, or *you* might suddenly recall something your own parents tried to tell you. This happens to every generation, and it happens to everyone who studies the Bible as well.

Overlooked evidence and evidentiary connection happen to every person. The more set in our ways that we are, the more difficult it is for evidence to be revealed to us.

Forming the Question

Questions are important to our understanding. There are those of us who ask questions and those of us who base life on being told what to do. When we fail to ask, then receiving answers is nearly impossible. Asking is not necessarily us asking another person a question, it is more about us forming a question within in our own mind. If we can't form the question in our mind, or if we refuse to do so, then we will not be able to recognize what could have been an answer even if we ourselves utter it to someone else, which is really quite common.

When Jesus said "ask and you shall receive", he was likely referring to something greater than our becoming aware. But it is equally likely that he also meant that when we have something formed in our mind, it is easier to receive or realize an answer to the question that we have adequately formed in our mind.

When it comes to Bible study, think about all the things discussed in this book and think about properly forming questions in your own mind. Consider all of the mental separations mentioned and the types of evidence and how that evidence fits with Scripture. Also, try to keep your mind focused on Old Testament "Scripture" because that is what the New Testament refers to when it mentions "Scripture".

Understanding these things helps to clear the path on our way to properly forming questions we may have about the Bible. We might question who Israel is, but if we don't see other specific information, then we are certain to misinterpret the Israelites. However, once we form the question properly in our mind then we can suddenly see the bigger picture.

Of all of the aspects of studying the Bible, *forming the question properly* in our mind is the single most important task for each of us to do.

The Gift of Wonder

Our ability to wonder is humanity's greatest gift. If you had no ability to wonder you would probably be dead because you wouldn't do things like wonder if a car is coming before you step into the street to cross it. You likely wouldn't see the differences between a living thing and a non-living thing, or something that is poisonous versus not poisonous.

Children are filled with wonder. You can see it in them the moment they open their eyes when they are born. They look about and *see* all that surrounds them and continuously take in that information. The moment they become mobile they put anything and everything they find immediately into their mouth to test it as they scamper around the house on their little expeditions.

When they are toddlers, they venture into anything to *discover*. A child's vast sense of discovery is unfocused and lacks direction, but as we age we gain mastery of this gift and can use it to learn whatever we desire to know; which in itself is very telling of the knowledge that is already within us.

When we come to some conclusion, that conclusion is us trying to fill in a blank or void in our knowledge. As we attempt to fill this information gap we speculate on what we think is likely true, or at least possible, and we then set out to prove that our speculation is correct. Unfortunately, all too often we *insist* we are correct as we twist any facts to fit our own theory.

Think about this for a moment. We are able to project in our minds accurate assumptions based upon information that we currently receive or experience, and then through those projections in our mind we determine what we might find and where we might find it. If we're cautious in our determinations, our sense of curiosity can cause us to properly form questions in our mind. When the answers are revealed to us, then more questions will arise and be properly formed in our mind, it is then that the floodgates of Truth begin to pour forth regarding your Biblical quests.

While we cannot pass on our knowledge to subsequent generations beyond the basics discussed in this book, we can pass on the methods of Truth so that our children's floodgates of Truth can also study the Bible when their time comes.

Chapter 24

Promises Kept

In the Bible there are many promises made to people. Some promises were directed to all people, and some were exclusively directed to "God's people", and some other promises were directed to specific individuals. But out of all of these promises, the most important one was the promise of Salvation which was made to Adam and Eve, and it applies the **all** of their offspring. If the Bible is a true book, then the Salvation commitment made to Adam and Eve applies to *everyone* who has ever lived, to *everyone* who is alive now, and to *everyone* who will ever live in the future, and all we need to do is to accept it and follow God's simple laws as established in the Bible.

Keeping the Bible's text as pure and as close to original as possible should always be everyone's goal. The words of the books in the Bible have actually never changed and they say what they say. However, when subsequent generations attempt to reinterpret the text, things often go wayward allowing for erroneous theories to arise. We can only hope to fully understand the promises made by the Creator if we are able grasp the basics of purest ancient Biblical texts. The starting point for that is a good and trustworthy Bible translation. Sadly, the wording in many modern translations allows for a great deal of scientific misinterpretation.

The words of the Bible should not change, but they do. If we try to mesh the Bible with things like big bang and Darwinian evolution, it takes away a great deal of meaning from some of God's promises that were addressed to all people. At some point regarding the entire Bible study and Bible reading issue, we each have to make a determination as to what we will believe about the evidence we find. Because, regardless of each our own final conclusions, there is the underlying truth of what actually occurred. If we are correct in our assessment of that history, then our conclusions will be correct, but if our assessments are wrong, then our conclusions will be wrong.

When our conclusions are wrong, it skews our chosen belief and might lead us to a bad outcome. Our mission is to find what is *accurate* in the Bible by looking at *all* of the scientific, archeological, geological, and Biblical evidence that surrounds us, and then make our determination about the validity of the truth of the Bible–a rare event for sure.

In this book, I hope that you have found some *tools to assist* in your quest to find solid answers to the questions you now have, and also for those questions that you will form as you continue to read or study the Bible.

Promises in the Book

Of all the books in the world, none have been as controversial as the text of the Tanakh–the Christian Bible's Old Testament. The difference between these two, Tanakh and Bible, again is basically the difference of the addition of the New Testament that details the Birth, Death, Resurrection, and Ascension of The Christ and the beginning of The Christ's Church, or the people who properly follow The Christ.

The Torah, or the first five books of the Bible (*Genesis, Exodus, Leviticus, Numbers,* and *Deuteronomy*) contain many promises, and the primary of those promises is the promise of Salvation. This is true regardless of whether you are reading the Jewish Tanakh or a Christian Bible and it can even be understood from reading the Muslim Quran. Both the Jews and Christians, and even the Muslims believe that a promise was made to Adam and Eve and then through Abraham, to save humanity from Satan's power.

The Word Of God

God promised Salvation by telling Adam and Eve, "I will send my Word to save you." This is reinforced in John 1:1 "In the beginning was the Word, and the Word was with God, and the Word was God. 2 The same was in the beginning with God. 3 All things were made by him: and without him was made nothing that was made."

This was mentioned earlier in the book, but it is worthy of repeating. The Bible is *not* The Word of God, *The Christis* **is** The Word of God. While the Bible does contain God's words, there is a difference between these two concepts of "word". It is surprising the difference it makes regarding our ability to view the Scriptures properly when we make a distinction between "God's Word" versus God's word**s**.

You will notice if you look for it in the Bible, that the "Word of God came and said..." or something to that effect. If the Word of God speaks, and those words are written in the Bible, that would certainly make those particular parts of the Bible "inspired". But the recorded *words spoken* by the **Word of God** are not the Word of God. You will find more than a few instances of the "Word of God" entity speaking to a people in the Bible, or more often, to a specific person. There are other references in the Bible that likely indicate the same "Word of God" entity but they are not specifically stated as "the Word of God said..."

The main *promise* in the Bible was to come through **the Word of God** which was explained through God's words at various points throughout the Bible.

The Bible

A Bible is a book of paper or papyrus originally exported from a coastal Mediterranean port-city called Byblos. This stack of papyrus or paper has in it many words grouped into many books. These books tell of the history of Salvation and how it came, beginning from Adam and Eve through all generations—until The Christ if you use a Christian Bible rather than a Jewish Tanakh. The Bible is not a book, it is a collection of documents that we call "books" that are bound together for convenience sake and are collectively called "The Bible" by most people. Not all Bibles have the same number of books in them, and not all "Bibles" have the New Testament. But *all* Bibles, and yes even the Quran, are connected to the Old Testament "Scriptures".

"God's people", as they are referred to in the Old Testament of the Bible, are still alive and well to this day, but most have lost their identity through thousands of years of assimilation. Then there are those who claim to be "God's People" but are not. And there are also those who claim to *not* be God's people but actually are.

One of the biggest, and I mean *the* biggest, misunderstandings about the Bible is that it somehow only applies to "God's people". This is not true in any sense of the Bible and it cannot be true or the Bible is utterly false. A holiday, such as Christmas, is not a "Christian" holiday. If Jesus The Christ is, in fact, the promised Savior, then "Christmas" and especially "Easter" or more appropriately "Resurrection Day" are holidays for *all humans* and all are invited into the celebration. Come-lately "holidays" that are celebrated around the same time as Christmas and Easter, are not necessarily wrong, but if they are *me-too* holidays, then they are a waste of time. They are a waste of time since Christmas is the arrival of the promised Savior and Easter celebrates the Resurrection of the Savior for **all** of mankind—that is to say **every** offspring of Adam and Eve for **all generations** evermore!

If the Bible is accurate, then Adam and Eve had children who expanded in quantity until the flood, but were then narrowed back down to only eight souls with Noah and his family. And if the Bible is to believed, then all of humanity that is alive today has descended from these eight people. And to be more concise, only from six of them since there are no indicators that Noah and his wife had any further offspring than his three sons Shem, Ham, and Japheth. When you read through the Bible, consider trying to follow the promises as those promises weave their way throughout the Bible. It is a very interesting path!

The Covenants

The Bible contains multiple covenants with different people throughout the Bible. The covenants were promises attached to agreements that God made with various people. The first obvious covenant that we think of is that of Salvation which was made with Adam and Eve, but there were also several other important covenants made. All of the Covenants had a stipulation for some sort of compliance on the part of mankind or on the part of the people or person that the covenant was made with.

These covenants were expanded when each new covenant was made. Most of the covenants followed a particular bloodline and were added to the first Salvation Covenant, with each addition creating a somewhat more detailed covenant. The primary check points for the covenants were Adam, Noah, Abraham, Isaac, Jacob, Moses, David, and Jesus. The covenants were frequently broke, but *they were broke by people*, never by God.

As far as the human side goes, probably the only covenant that was not breeched by a person was the Salvation covenant when the Son of Man, that is to say Jesus The Christ, accepted death on the Cross. He could easily have run away and defied his purpose, but according to the Gospels, he did not.

The eternal promise that was added to throughout the Bible and was made to all mankind was that: through Truth, life could continue so that we could all achieve eternal life through the Savior and through the Salvation that He bought and brought for all so that all mankind could become whole with God once again.

Are We Holy?

There's so much good information lost in words in our modern culture, and it keeps getting worse as language progressively deteriorates. Some people claim that English is a "living language", and it is true in that it changes, and in that way it is alive. But I contend that with every deviation from the true root of a word, the English language dies a little bit more, losing its value bit by bit as we pervert it and use it in vain.

There are many words that can be better understood when we take the time to grasp their underlying intent. One of those words is "Holy". What is "Holy"? And who is *Holy*? Some of us certainly act "holier than thou", but we don't even know what the word is describing.

The term "holy" is used frequently in the Bible. In fact, it can be found hundreds of times. It is one of the top words that is not an *and*, *the*, or *with* type word. *Holy* is not a word you use in a typical sentence, unless you are speaking of God or something connected to God. The root of "Holy" is ultimately *whole* or *complete*. It is a state of perfection of the object of the discussion. God is "Holy" according to the Bible, which makes sense since God is The Creator, as is indicated in the Bible. And many things in the Bible were to be holy or would become holy. This was an indication of completeness or fullness or perfection. God wanted his people to be a "Holy people" and said that "they would be called a Holy People, the Redeemed of the Lord" in Isaiah 62:12.

We are to be a Holy people according to this when we are "Redeemed of the Lord". If this "Bible" that we study is accurate and if it is true, it means that people are supposed to be Holy when redeemed, but only when **we choose** redemption. But, is this for the people referred to as "God's People" alone, or is it for all of mankind? Look into it for yourself and see what you determine.

Revelation 4:8 "Holy, Holy, Holy, is the Lord God Almighty, who was and is and is to come!" indicates a fullness and a completeness of this "God" of the Bible who is the God of Abraham and Ismael and the God of Abraham, Isaac, and Jacob. The Bible is unmistakably clear in its indication of a Creator-God and of miracles and of Salvation. Our job is to legitimately discredit the Bible with Truth, or legitimately prove it with Truth to ourselves and to others.

It is rather entertaining watching people refute the Bible as an act of rebellion as they unsuccessfully attempt to discredit the Bible. In our modern high-tech culture, we are praised and applauded for our clever but often weak arguments against the Bible.

But if you really want to rebel against the grain of society and ruffle people's feathers and feel the resistance, stop with all of the foolish rebellious behavior and modifications of self that foul your body and...

Be a real Rebel and read the Bible,

and then tell your friends about it!

UNDERSTANDING THE CHURCH

Upon This Rock I Will Build My Church

Church in the Lurch - a House Built Upon Sand

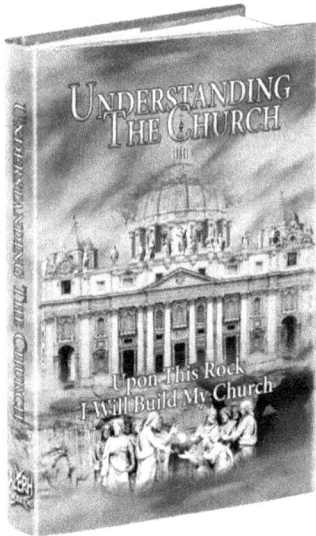

The Church is rapidly dying, and much of the clergy in recent times have been doing it more harm than good. People are fleeing from the Churches as they seek a religious perspective that fits a modern worldview. Should we revive this old Church and try to save it from its own demise? What exactly is "The Church", and who or which of the many religions is the official caretaker of it?

The Christian religions of the world have done their fair share of damage to themselves and to the world, but in the bigger picture, they have done more good than damage. Saving the Church is probably worth our collective efforts because the Churches are perhaps the most charitable group of organizations that existed throughout history and even up to today.

The main reason that the Churches are in the rough condition that they are today is due to a lack of understanding by clergy and congregation. We can overcome this dark era of the Church and revive it only through *Understanding The Church*.

Understanding The Church will help you in Bible study, or even to simply better understand the Church. But most importantly, *Understanding The Church — Upon This Rock I Will Build My Church* will help to revive this dying patient.

Search: Understanding The Church Book
SayItBooks.com

Rock the Boat with Layers of Truth

Do you believe that the entire world flooded roughly four thousand years ago and that a man named Noah built a large boat to save a small remnant of human and animal life that would repopulate the entire Earth? This is the belief of many Christians, Jews, and Muslims, but then we have those who believe that the entire story was written thousands of years ago for entertainment only.

Could either case be true? Is either realistic? After all there is a lot of evidence of catastrophic worldwide flooding. But then there are those making the point that there's not enough water on Earth to cover the mountains. So, which, if either, is it? If either case were proven to be undeniably true it would have major impact on opposing perspectives. If it never occurred, it would devastate most Bible-based religions. But how would it affect modern sciences if it was proven true? It would force every scientist to face a reality for which they have not been educated.

Take a journey through these and other Biblical flood questions and consider the perspectives presented in *The Science Of God Volume 5 – Boats, Floods, and Noah – The Deluge*, a truly logical scientific explanation of the viability regarding the Biblical flood of Noah's time.

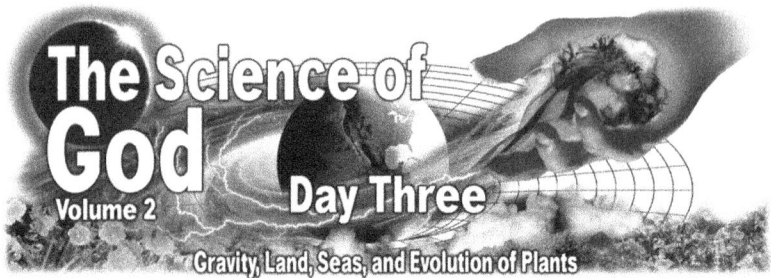

Volume 1 - The First Four Days

Is there a God? Did we evolve? Did everything start from a big bang? These questions have been plaguing our minds for many years. Only science-minded people and clergy seem to have the answers. But do they really have any true answers?

Is what we are told by science true? Is what we are told by the Church true? Or are there other better explanations for everything? Did we hitch a ride from Mars, or is that all fantasy science? Was everything created in six twenty-four hour days, or did it all take billions of years to happen? Few people are willing to even fully consider these questions, and even fewer have any coherent answers. *The Science of God Volume 1 – The First Four Days* challenges your current beliefs while asking tough questions of science and of the Church.

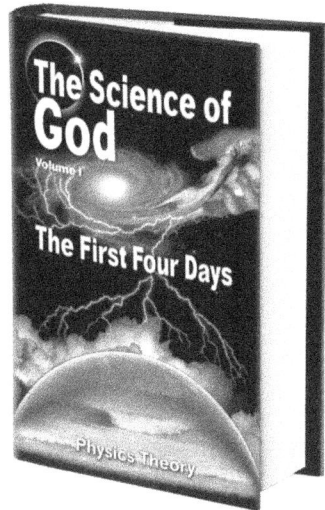

For years, Christian after Christian has attempted to argue for God and the Bible's Creation only to fail miserably. Why is this, why is it that Christians cannot seem to win this debate? Often Christians think they are winning the debate only to find themselves at a loss to answer the real questions, and then they get mocked for their poor answers.

Whether you are a scientist or an average Christian and want to discuss the Creation debate, *The Science of God Volume 1 – The First Four Days* is a mandatory read for you. *The Science of God* takes you through the thought process to enable you to speak intelligibly about Creation, the cosmos, evolution, and astrophysics.

Search: The Science Of God Book Volume 1
SayItBooks.com

The Prayer How-To Manual
Understanding Prayer
Why Our Prayers Don't Work

Learn the Real Secret of Prayer

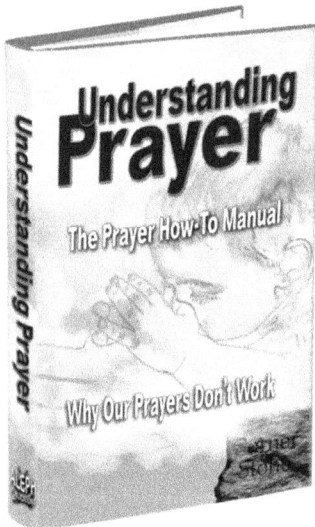

There's a secret that many have tried to understand but failed to accomplish. We pray day after day after day with little or no positive results, causing us to lose faith.

Some people believe that there's a secret method that must be followed to get your prayers answered and receive the things you want in life, but their success is limited, if it comes at all; while others believe that they're not worthy to have their prayers answered. Few people know the True secret, and when they tell us we often misunderstand them.

Understanding Prayer explains, in easy to grasp language, the mysteries behind many causes of prayer failure. True success in your prayers is not measured by how often you pray, how long you pray, or even how badly you want something and how hard you for pray it. True success in your prayer life is measured by *results*!

Understanding Prayer offers you the opportunity to get those results as it reveals the mysteries of a full and robust prayerful connection allowing you solid and repeatable results nearly on command. A little time to read and pray is all it takes to quickly put these sound, true, simple principles to work for you and your family. Gain the understanding of prayer and of how to receive the blessings of financial and mental wealth that can benefit you and keep you free from strife and trouble for years to come!

Search: Understanding Prayer Book
SayItBooks.com

Notes

Notes

Notes

Notes

www.ingramcontent.com/pod-product-compliance
Lightning Source LLC
Chambersburg PA
CBHW030822090426
42737CB00009B/839